COLLECTOR'S VALUE GUIDE

DIGIMON™

Collector Handbook and Price Guide

PREMIERE EDITION

Digimon™

The Collector's Value Guide™ is not sponsored by, or otherwise affiliated with, Bandai or its licensees. Any opinions expressed are solely those of the authors, and do not necessarily reflect those of Bandai or its licensees.

Front cover (left to right, from top): "Tai & Koromon™" *(American Trading Card);* "MetalGreymon™" *(5-inch Digivolving Action Figure);* "Patamon™" *(5-inch Digivolving Action Figure);* "Etemon™" *(Japanese Battle Card).*

Back cover (left to right): "WereGarurumon™" *(5-inch Digivolving Action Figure);* "Gomamon™" *(American Trading Card).*

EDITORIAL

Managing Editor: Jeff Mahony
Associate Editors: Melissa A. Bennett
Jan Cronan
Gia C. Manalio
Paula Stuckart
Contributing Editor: Mike Micciulla
Assistant Editors: Heather N. Carreiro
Jennifer Filipek
Joan C. Wheal
Editorial Assistants: Jennifer Abel
Timothy R. Affleck
Beth Hackett
Christina M. Sette
Steven Shinkaruk

WEB (collectorbee.com)

Web Reporter: Samantha Bouffard
Web Graphic Designer: Ryan Falis

R&D

R&D Specialist: Priscilla Berthiaume
R&D Graphic Designer: Angi Shearstone

ART

Creative Director: Joe T. Nguyen
Assistant Art Director: Lance Doyle
Senior Graphic Designers: Susannah C. Judd
David S. Maloney
Carole Mattia-Slater
David Ten Eyck
Graphic Designers: Jennifer J. Bennett
Sean-Ryan Dudley
Kimberly Eastman
Marla B. Gladstone
Caryn Johnson
Jim MacLeod
Jeremy Maendel
Chery-Ann Poudrier

PRODUCTION

Production Manager: Scott Sierakowski
Product Development Manager: Paul Rasid

ISBN 1-585-98058-7

CHECKERBEE™ and COLLECTOR'S VALUE GUIDE™ are trademarks of CheckerBee, Inc.
Copyright © 2000 by CheckerBee, Inc.
All rights reserved. No part of this book may be reproduced or transmitted in any form or by any means, electronic or mechanical, including photocopying, recording, or by any information storage or retrieval system, without the written permission of the publisher.

CheckerBee PUBLISHING
306 Industrial Park Road
Middletown, CT 06457

Table Of Contents

Introducing The Collector's Value Guide • 5

Digimon™ Digest: A Look At The Phenomenon • 6

Digimon™ Character Guide • 10

A Closer Look At The Television Show • 18

How To Read A Battle Card • 24

How To Play The Battle Card Game • 26

MVC: The Most Valuable Cards • 29

How To Use Your Value Guide • 30

Battle Card Starter Set • 31

Battle Card Starter Set Version 2 • 47

Booster Card Series 1 & 2 • 56

Booster Card Series 3 • 84

American Trading Cards • 96

Trading Collection Light Series 1 • 111

Trading Collection Light Series 2 • 118

Table Of Contents

Other American and Japanese Cards • 132

Future Releases • 136

Total Value Of My Collection • 138

The Pro-Digi-ous Secondary Market • 140

Digimon™ Is Everywhere! • 141

Digi-Dictionary • 148

Digimon™ American Card Checklist • 149

Index • 153

Introducing The Collector's Value Guide™

Welcome to the first edition of the Collector's Value Guide™ to Digimon™. Whether you have been collecting Digimon since the first virtual pets were introduced, or have just become aware of the phenomenon with the cards and cartoon, the Collector's Value Guide™ will lead you through the wonderful Digi-world of collectibles.

Digimon has captured the imaginations of children everywhere with its magnificent monsters and thoughtful storylines. The introduction of the collectible Digi-Battle Card Game has excited card collectors and older fans, as well.

The Collector's Value Guide™ is your one complete source for a wealth of Digi-knowledge. Inside these pages you will find complete information about the red-hot American and Japanese cards, used for both battle and trading. Other great features found within include:

- Profiles of the eight kids and their Digimon
- A history of Digimon from its virtual pet origins to today
- A guide to the television series
- Rules and tips for mastering the card game
- An in-depth look at other Digimon products ranging from clothes to toys
- Values for American and Japanese battle and trading cards
- A look at the most valuable cards
- And much, much more!

Digimon™ Digest:
A Look At The Phenomenon

Here comes the latest craze – Digimon! Those already familiar with the smash-hit Fox Kids animated program "Digimon: Digital Monsters" know that Digimon is the latest and greatest in imported Japanese entertainment, but they may not know that Digimon actually got its start as a hand-held interactive virtual pet and not as a television show.

Digimon was the brainchild of the Japan-based Bandai Co., which developed Digimon as a successor to its popular Tamagotchi virtual pets. The Digimon digital pet premiered in Japan in 1997, and immediately attracted a large following. In early 1998, Bandai brought Digimon to the United States where it enjoyed steady success. In fact, in February of 1998, the Digimon virtual pet was ranked by a national toy retail tracking service as the fourth highest-selling toy of the month.

As the popularity of Digimon grew, web sites sprang up all over the Internet filled with growth charts, cheats, tips, codes and instructions on how to raise and train Digital Monsters. Various versions of Digimon were introduced that featured different monsters with varying "Digi-volving" capabilities. Without a doubt, much of the appeal of Digimon lay in its exclusive "dock n' rock" feature, which allowed two Digimon owners to let their monsters duke it out with each other by connecting their devices together. The way in which Digimon are raised determines what kind of a fighter it will become. Those who trained their Digital Monsters well and

fed and rested them on a regular schedule could get an Ultimate fighter such as MetalGreymon. Those who neglected their Digimon could end up with a useless Digimon like Numemon.

Digimon™ Hits The Airwaves

As U.S. children (and grown-ups) happily played with their Digimon virtual pets, back in Japan, the Digimon phenomenon was going into new territory. On March 7, 1999, "Digimon Adventure" (produced by Toei Animation) premiered on Japanese television. The anime series took the original digital monsters and plopped them into an animated Digi-world, moving way beyond the original concept into an action-filled, plot-driven half hour of great entertainment. Around the same time, Toei released a short film, also called "Digimon Adventure," which featured a younger Taichi Kamiya (a character in the television series) and his little sister Hikari.

What happened next was unusual. Saban Entertainment, which brought North Americans such mega-hits as "The Mighty Morphin Power Rangers," bought the rights to the animated Digimon series and premiered it on the Fox Kids network in the United States on August 14, 1999, only five months after its initial release in Japan. This quick turnaround to U.S. television was rare for a Japanese animated series, which usually has at least a full season's run in its home country before being shipped abroad.

The show, called "Digimon: Digital Monsters" in the United States, was altered slightly for a Western audience, but remained largely true to the original Japanese series. It focuses on a group of kids away at summer camp who are transported to a parallel world, the Digi-world, to save it (and the real world) from evil forces. Each child acquires a Digital Monster companion who serves as a friend, mentor and protector, Digi-volving into a larger and stronger form when its human friend is in danger.

"Digimon: Digital Monsters" immediately caught on, spawning fan-driven web sites devoted to the show and even "shrines" dedicated to certain characters. Episodes were discussed in detail, with fans eagerly awaiting each new one. Before long, "Digimon" was the highest-rated show on the Fox Kids lineup, and its popularity can be attested to by the fact that it is shown every weekday afternoon and twice on Saturdays.

New Branches On The Digimon™ Product Tree

Hot on the heels of the television series came a line of products to satisfy the cravings of those Digi-fanatics who just couldn't get enough of their Digimon. Bandai teamed up with the U.S. trading card company Upper Deck to introduce trading cards based on the TV show as well as a Digi-Battle collectible card game. Action figures and fingerboards based on the show have also hit stores. This is just the tip of the iceberg. Digimon is still so relatively new, even in Japan, that we are just beginning to see the flood of Digimon merchandise and collectibles. For instance, a Sony PlayStation game, "Digimon World," is in the works and Saban Entertainment has recently greenlighted the release of a motion picture based on the television show for U.S. audiences.

And that's not all. Continuing in the virtual pet tradition, Bandai is releasing the Digivice, a hand-held game that lets players choose one of the Digi-destined's Digimon from the show to help them battle evil Digimon. Additionally, booster sets continue to be added to the Digi-Battle card game, and Saban has purchased the second season of "Digimon: Digital Monsters" episodes to be broadcast in the United States. The second season of "Digimon" features new kids and Digimon, along with our old favorites.

THE LURE OF DIGIMON™

So what's the appeal of Digimon? What keeps us tuning in day after day, week after week, to see what new adventures our heroes and heroines will embark on next? Well, for starters, the characters act like real kids, and we can identify with them. What kid hasn't dreamed of going on an exciting adventure with his or her friends (and missing a lot of school)? Plus, the human characters aren't perfect. The kids have their own set of issues that they're dealing with, and they don't always make the right decisions or behave in the most admirable way. Mimi can be shallow, Matt is sometimes argumentative and moody and Tai often forgets to look before he leaps. Despite their shortcomings, they all strive to work as a team and they all care about and depend on one another.

Of course, we can't overlook the Digital Monsters themselves. From the cute In-Training Digimon to the battle-ready Ultimate Digimon, these monsters are just awesome! Who wouldn't like to have a personal Digimon that Digi-volves into a ferocious form to protect its human companion? Fan favorites such as WereGarurumon, Angemon and MetalGreymon are just as exciting to watch in action as adorable Digimon like Palmon and Patamon. Plus, Digimon are great items to collect, as they can be purchased as cards, plush and figurines.

Digimon truly offers something for everyone, and the fun is definitely just getting started! So head to the Digi-world and join in the adventure of a lifetime!

COLLECTOR'S
VALUE GUIDE™

Digimon™ Character Guide

With over 200 Digimon and eight humans populating the Digi-landscape, you will find a character guide to be just as necessary as a map. Let these pages be your guide in determining friend from foe.

We start out with a look at the human characters and their companion Digimon. The companion Digimon are displayed in all their Digi-volved forms, starting with the novice, or "In-Training," Digimon and continuing through all of their evolutions. The crests that represent different aspects of the Digi-destined kids' personalities are displayed in the upper-right hand corner of their pictures.

The later part of this section serves as a quick visual guide to some of the more prominent characters in the Digi-world, from Andromon to Woodmon and nearly everyone in between.

Taichi "Tai" Kamiya™

Tai is a natural leader with an adventurous and exuberant nature. Back in the real world, his athletic and leadership abilities were displayed on the soccer field, but in the Digi-world, he needs to put those skills to use for survival. Although he is courageous, which earns him the Crest of Courage, Tai can act rashly, putting himself and the rest of the group in danger. With the help of his In-Training Digimon – Koromon – Tai is learning to be a mature and responsible leader, but that doesn't mean he won't make some mistakes along the way!

Koromon™
Koromon is an In-Training Digimon who befriends Tai when he first arrives in the Digital World.

Agumon™
This friendly and protective Rookie Digimon uses its Pepper Breath Attack to send smoke signals as well as to fight.

Greymon™
This powerful Champion comes to the rescue when the kids are in trouble. Its fiery Nova Blast makes it a fierce foe!

MetalGreymon™
Watch out for this Ultimate Digimon's vaporizing Giga Blaster!

WarGreymon™
Agumon Digi-volved into WarGreymon in the "Prophecy" episode of "Digimon: Digital Monsters."

Sora Takenouchi™

An irrepressible tomboy, Sora is also mature and responsible. She often acts as a big sister to the other Digi-destined, and is the most serious of the group. Don't get the impression that Sora doesn't like to have fun, though – she would love to run around the Digital World without a care and have a great adventure – but the safety and well-being of the others is always foremost in her mind. Because of her compassionate and caring nature, Sora holds the Crest of Love.

Yokomon™
This In-Training Digimon is very brave, despite its small size. Kind and polite, Yokomon and Sora make a good team.

Biyomon™
A child-like Rookie, Biyomon has a calming effect on Sora, helping to ease the burden of her responsibilities.

Birdramon™
This Champion evolves when Sora is in danger. With the Meteor Wing attack, Birdramon won't let anything hurt Sora.

Garudamon™
Ultimate Digimon Garudamon is a mighty guardian of the sky with an impressive Wing Blade attack.

Yamato "Matt" Ishida™

Matt is one cool character. He's a rebel with an attitude, and no one is going to tell him what to do! Beneath his icy exterior, however, lurks a sensitive and introspective soul who will do anything to protect his younger half-brother T.K. Matt's a loner, and has trouble expressing his feelings, but he really does care for his fellow Digi-destined, despite his frequent tiffs with Tai. When his friends need him, Matt will always be there and this loyalty has earned him the Crest of Friendship.

Tsunomon™
Tsunomon is Matt's In-Training Digimon. Tsunomon is the quiet type, like Matt, but a brave and loyal companion.

Gabumon™
This Rookie serves as a mentor to Matt and is also a fearsome protector whose Blue Blaster can ice the enemy.

Garurumon™
No one wants to be on the receiving end of this Champion Digimon's Howling Blaster attack.

Were-Garurumon™
This Ultimate Digimon uses ferocious kicks and punches to defend the Digi-destined.

Metal-Garurumon™
MetalGarurumon uses the Metal Wolf Claw attack to freeze its enemies and break them to pieces.

COLLECTOR'S VALUE GUIDE™

Mimi Tachikawa™

Mimi is the "princess" of the group. She's been pampered her entire life and never knew the slightest bit of hardship before her arrival in the Digital World. Although Mimi is without a doubt spoiled and self-centered, she's not selfish. She may be overconcerned with her appearance, a bit of a complainer and slightly oblivious to the world around her, but she truly cares for her friends and doesn't have a mean-spirited bone in her body. For these reasons, Mimi has earned the Crest of Sincerity.

Tanemon™
Tanemon is a plant-like In-Training Digimon with a sweet disposition.

Palmon™
Rookie Palmon helps Mimi to see outside of herself and care for others. Mimi loves sharing girl talk with Palmon.

Togemon™
This Champion Digimon resembles a cactus. Its Needle Spray helps the kids get out of prickly situations.

Lillymon™
Don't let the small size of this Ultimate Digimon fool you — its Flower Cannon packs a wallop.

Koushiro "Izzy" Izumi™

The computer-whiz and all-around brain of the gang, Izzy is never far from his laptop computer. Izzy is intensely curious, and the secrets of the Digital World are, to him, a puzzle that must be solved – with the help of technology, of course. On the other hand, Izzy sometimes becomes too wrapped up in his own world to realize the danger that he or his friends are in. Many of the mysteries of the Digital World are unlocked due to Izzy's diligence and intelligence. Appropriately, Izzy holds the Crest of Knowledge.

Motimon™
The In-Training Motimon, with its knowledge of the Digi-world, is a perfect companion for the curious Izzy.

Tentomon™
This Rookie helps Izzy to focus his knowledge. Its Super Shocker attack is nothing short of electric!

Kabuterimon™
Winged Champion Kabuterimon helps get the kids out of sticky situations with its Electro Shocker attack.

Mega-Kabuterimon™
Mega-Kabuterimon saved Izzy from the evil Vademon by using its Horn Buster attack.

Hercules-Kabuterimon™
This Mega-level Digimon attacks with the one-two punch of Mega Electro Shocker and Giga Scissor Claw.

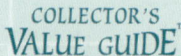

Joe Kido™

Nervous and studious, Joe is also a first-class worrywart. He's fearful about missing too much school, and he's constantly afraid of what's around the next bend. Joe has a tendency to think the worst about situations, and his foremost concern is for the safety of himself and his friends. He relies on reason to get out of tough situations, which can be a good thing, considering the rashness of some of the other Digi-destined! Despite his fears and phobias, Joe is steady and reliable, earning him the Crest of Reliability.

Bukamon™
Bukamon's funny and carefree personality contrasts with Joe's serious demeanor.

Gomamon™
This Rookie is a happy-go-lucky Digimon who helps Joe to lighten up and look at the bright side of things.

Ikkakumon™
The horned Champion Ikkakumon has a powerful Harpoon Torpedo attack that works on land or in water.

Zudomon™
All foes should beware of Ikkakumon's giant Vulcan's Hammer.

Hikari "Kari" Kamiya™

Kari is Tai's little sister and joined the Digi-destined team later than the others. She is the prophesied Eighth Child who will help to bring peace to the Digital World. Even though she was a latecomer, she is an essential part of the group. Kari is wise and compassionate beyond her years, but sometimes lets her empathy get in the way of her better judgment. Kari holds the Crest of Light.

Nyaromon™
Nyaromon is Kari's In-Training companion.

Salamon™
Rookie Salamon is the form that Angewomon Digi-volved to after battling Venom-Myotismon.

Gatomon™
This Champion once worked for the evil Myotismon, but once Kari appeared, Gatoman realized its true calling.

Angewomon™
This Ultimate Digimon has the ability to draw power from other Digimon and concentrate it into the Celestial Arrow.

Digimon™ Character Guide

COLLECTOR'S VALUE GUIDE™

13

Digimon™ Character Guide

Takeru "T.K." Takaishi™

T.K. is a generous and sweet little boy caught in a sometimes frightening world. Despite this, T.K. tries to be brave and he can usually hold his own in the Digital World. He looks up to his big brother Matt, and tries to be like him. Although T.K. tries his best to stay strong, the life-threatening events he must face every day can get the better of him, and he has been known to dissolve into tears on occasion. T.K.'s Rookie Digimon, Patamon, is a playmate and nurturing parental substitute for T.K., who needs a little extra encouragement at times. T.K.'s innocence has earned him the Crest of Hope.

Tokomon™
Little Tokomon, an In-Training Digimon, is T.K.'s buddy as well as a nurturing parental substitute for the young boy.

Patamon™
This Rookie watches over and plays with T.K. Its Boom Bubble attack is quite effective!

Angemon™
Angemon is the strongest Digimon of them all! He defeated the evil Devimon with his Hand of Fate.

Magna-Angemon™
This Digimon is a fierce warrior who fights for justice against the evil forces of the Digi-world.

Other Prominent Digimon™

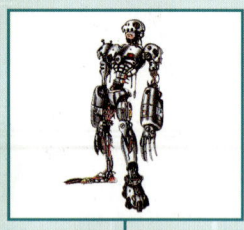

Andromon™

Apemon™

Bakemon™

Candlemon™

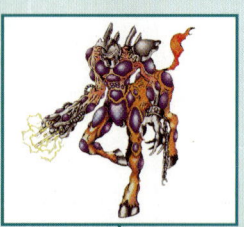

Centarumon™

Coelamon™

COLLECTOR'S VALUE GUIDE™

Digimon™ Character Guide

DemiDevimon™

Devimon™

Dokugumon™

Dolphmon™

Frigimon™

Gekomon™

Gotsumon™

Kimeramon™

Kunemon™

LadyDevimon™

Leomon™

Mammothmon™

MarineDevimon™

MegaSeadramon™

Meramon™

COLLECTOR'S VALUE GUIDE™

Digimon™ Character Guide

MetalEtemon™

Monochromon™

Monzaemon™

Musyamon™

Myotismon™

Nanimon™

Octomon™

Ogremon™

Okuwamon™

Otamamon™

Piedmon™

Piximon™

Pukumon™

Pumpkinmon™

Puppetmon™

COLLECTOR'S VALUE GUIDE™

Digimon™ Character Guide

RedVegiemon™

Rockmon™

SaberLeomon™

Seadramon™

ShogunGekomon™

SkullGreymon™

SkullMeramon™

Starmon™

Sukamon™

Tyrannomon™

Unimon™

VenomMyotismon™

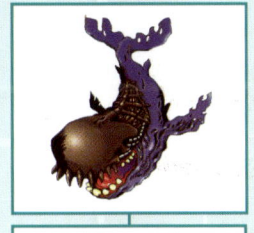
Whamon™

Wizardmon™

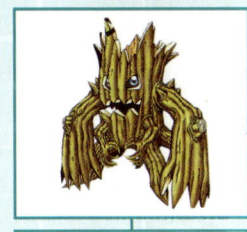
Woodmon™

COLLECTOR'S
VALUE GUIDE™

A Closer Look At The Television Show

Since premiering in August 1999 on the Fox Kids network, "Digimon: Digital Monsters" has kept both boys and girls glued to their television sets for each episodic adventure of animated Digi-delight. How did this popular series come to be? The answers lie not on File Island, hidden among the wild Digimon, but in the talented animation studios of Japan.

The Digimon animated series was developed in Japan by Toei Animation, and it debuted in the spring of 1999. Sensing a hot property of monstrous proportions, Saban Entertainment worked hard to quickly prepare the program for U.S. audiences. When it started airing on the Fox Kids network, "Digimon" soon became its highest-rated show.

BEHIND THE SCENES

Preparing an animated Japanese show for U.S. audiences is no simple task. Fox Kids is responsible for translating the episodes into English and reworking the plots for Western sensibilities. Japanese elements considered out of place on U.S. television sets are left on the cutting room floor. Dialogue is rewritten with the doubly difficult task of staying true to the plot and also having the words match the mouth movements of the characters. When this has been completed, the episode is ready to air on U.S. television.

Not content with taking over the United States and Japan, Digimon is set to become a global phenomenon. The program is a ratings success in Canada and will soon be airing in the United Kingdom, France and Latin America.

THE STORY THUS FAR

The Digimon cartoon follows the adventures of Tai, Sora, Matt, T.K., Izzy, Mimi, Joe (and later, Kari) as they brave the strange land known as the Digi-world. The kids are swept away from summer camp to the Digi-world (a fate many children would also welcome), where they first find their Digi-vices and meet the Digimon in their In-Training forms. The seven children and the seven In-Training Digimon quickly bond with each other, and then their adventures begin in earnest.

The kids soon learn that the In-Training Digimon do not stay helpless little blobs for long. They Digi-volve into incredibly awesome new forms that are able to repel the evil Digimon (and there are many) that wish to harm the seven kids.

But are all of these fearsome antagonists truly bad guys? A strange black device is found embedded in the back of the raging Meramon, who had once been the peaceful guardian of Mount Miharashi. When the device is removed, Meramon regains its senses. The discovery of this Black Gear leads the kids on the trail of the evil mastermind Devimon, the black-hearted force behind the corrupted Digimon.

Devimon rules over File Island's demon underworld, brainwashing good Digimon by inserting the Black Gears into their bodies, thereby placing them under its control. Devimon's evil plan is to take over File Island, and then the world! It uses the Touch of Evil attack and the Black Gear–infected Digimon against the Digi-destined kids, hoping to destroy them. Unfortunately for Devimon, Patamon (T.K.'s Digimon) Digi-volves into Angemon, destroying the villainous creature and sabotaging its nefarious plans.

A Trip To Server

Defeating Devimon takes every last ounce of their strength and courage, but the Digi-destined don't rest on their laurels. Soon, they set out for the continent of Server, where they face the rockin' and rollin', Elvis-impersonating Etemon and its Dark Network. The Digi-destined went to Server to locate their crests and tags, but Etemon is determined to destroy the children and use their crests and tags for its own evil purposes. It uses its Dark Network Concert Crash attack to stop the kids' Digimon from Digi-volving (and also to annoy anyone who happens to be nearby). Etemon is eventually defeated by MetalGreymon, but you can't keep a bad rock star down, and it soon was on the comeback trail, this time in its ultimate form – MetalEtemon.

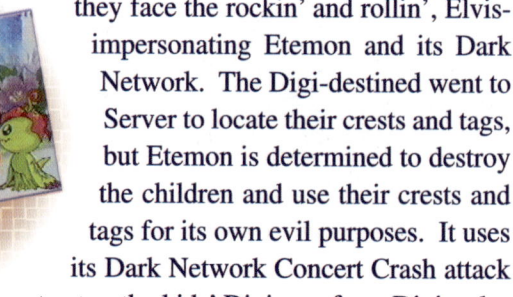

The continent of Server is also the place where the kids meet the mysterious Gennai. Not quite human but not quite Digimon, Gennai often appears out of nowhere to mentor the children and reveal to them bits of wisdom that will aid in their roles as the Digi-destined.

Trouble is never far off in the Digital World, and the bat-loving, vampiric Myotismon is the next enemy of the Digi-destined. This evil Digimon is searching for the prophesied eighth Digi-destined child – a child who turns out to be Tai's sister Kari! With DemiDevimon as its evil henchman, it opens a portal into the real world to search for and capture the eighth Digi-destined. The struggle to save Kari is an adventure that spans the real world and the Digi-world, with the fate of both hanging in the balance. Kari's Digimon turns out to be Gatomon, a Digimon who had been working in the service of Myotismon. Gatomon turns against Myotismon, and defeats him by Digi-volving into Angewomon.

Although seemingly vanquished, Myotismon returns as a terrifying new form called VenomMyotismon, thus fulfilling part of the prophecy that had been discovered by Gennai. This horrible vampire Digimon eats DemiDevimon to gain energy and prepares to wreak havoc on the world, but is ultimately defeated by the combined strength of WarGreymon and MetalGarurumon.

DemiDevimon, before its untimely demise at the hands – make that mouth – of VenomMyotismon, is quite a menace to the Digi-destined as well. As Myotismon's loyal henchman, DemiDevimon carries out diabolical plans and attempts to thwart the Digi-destined at every turn. This bat-like Digimon is a master of trickery whose misdeeds range from making Sora believe her crest will never glow again to convincing T.K. that Matt has left him and doesn't like him anymore. DemiDevimon's attempts at mischief are foiled, however, and it proves more of a nuisance than a real threat.

THE DARK MASTERS

After defeating VenomMyotismon, the Digi-destined return to the Digital World and find it in chaos. A new menace has arisen in their absence in the form of the four Dark Masters – MetalSeadramon, Machinedramon, Puppetmon and Piedmon. These

four evil beings have hatched a plot to take over the Digital World and destroy the Digi-destined, and it is up to the eight children to stop them. At first, the kids are defeated by MetalSeadramon, an Ultimate-level Digimon that proves to be more than a match for the kids' Champions. The tide of battle turns, however, and MetalSeadramon is the first Dark Master to be defeated, although

Whamon, a good Digimon who has always been loyal to the Digi-destined, is unfortunately sacrificed in the process.

Machinedramon is the second Dark Master to battle the Digi-destined. This mechanical monstrosity nearly pulverizes Tai and his companions. Machinedramon has a wide range of weapons available at its long fingertips, and can also call on its Metal Empire Army to scour the entire Digi-world in search of its prey. If Machinedramon had a heart, it would be as cold as steel.

Dark Master Puppetmon soon emerges as the kids' most persistent nemesis. Puppetmon is a fiendish puppet-like Digimon who can control both Digimon and the Digi-destined with its puppet strings. It lives in a mansion in the forest, surrounded by henchman who have to do its bidding and serve as its "playmates." Puppetmon loves to toy with others, playing evil games and tricks on the Digi-destined and their Digimon. Puppetmon is a tough opponent, but with the help of Matt and faithful WereGarurumon, it is finally defeated.

There's no rest for the weary Digi-destined, as, plotting and scheming from a castle on Spiral Mountain, the Dark Master Piedmon awaits the challenge of the eight kids. Although dressed like a jovial jester, evil Piedmon proves to be no laughing matter. With its fearsome swords and the ability to transform foes into harmless dolls, Piedmon comes close to defeating Tai and his friends. It is only through the heroic efforts of Piximon that the threat of Piedmon is temporarily thwarted and the Digi-destined live to fight another day. Tai and the others cannot relax for long, because Piedmon returns and almost has the last laugh, until Angemon Digi-volves into the mighty MagnaAngemon and defeats Piedmon for good.

What Happens Next?

While the fates of the current Digi-destined are still unknown to U.S. audiences, a second season has already begun airing in Japan. Titled "Digimon Adventures 02," this series introduces a new group of kids, while retaining some of the old favorites. Saban plans to release this series in the United States, so keep checking your local television listings.

Silver Screen Digimon

Television screens are proving to be too small to hold all the excitement that Digimon provides. You might just see "Digimon: The Movie" heading to your local theater! The success of the cartoon in Japan led to the release of two short theatrical features. There is a good chance that these shorts may be combined in a direct-to-video release in the United States. Twentieth Century Fox recently acquired the right to distribute Digimon films in the United States, so don't be surprised if Hollywood seems like "Digi-wood" in the near future.

How To Read A Battle Card

In order to fully master the Digi-Battle Card Game, you need to know your Digimon! Watching the television show, unfortunately, is not enough. You need to be familiar with the information found on each card. A well-informed player is a winning player, so it's vital to learn the components of a card.

1. This box indicates the card's Battle Type (red, green or yellow).

2. There are several requirements necessary to Digi-volve to a new character and they are listed here.

3. Digimon come in several levels – Rookie, Champion, Ultimate or Mega. You can learn what level your Digimon is here.

4. This number and letter combination indicates what number a card is in a particular set. Starter Set cards are preceded by the letters "St." Booster Set cards are preceded by the letters "Bo."

5. All 1st Edition cards are marked as such (American cards only).

6. There are over 20 different Digimon Groups; the one your character belongs to is listed here.

7. Digimon come in four different Types – either Data, Unclassified, Vaccine or Virus, and that information can be found in this box.

8. This box lists your Digimon's Special Ability. Digimon found in the Starter Set have the abilities of either Swim, Fly or Dig.

9. Special Effects are cited here. They provide bonuses when you do things such as win a match or Digi-volve to a new level.

10. There are three Power Techniques found on each card. The one you get to use is decided by your opponent's Battle Type.

11. The points you receive for defeating an opponent of a particular Digi-volve level are found here (American cards only).

12. The power of your Digimon is listed here. Power is decided by your opponent's Battle Type.

13. All Digimon in the same "family tree" have the same kind of background. Keep this in mind when choosing cards for your deck.

14. Character name.

15. This is the Lost Points box. In the Japanese version, players start out with an equal number of points, and then deduct "lost points" as they lose battles to opponents of a particular Digi-volve level (Japanese cards only).

16. On the Japanese cards, the Digimon have quotes to inspire players during battle (Japanese cards only).

How To Play
The Battle Card Game

The Digi-Battle Card Game gives players the opportunity to battle their Digimon head-to-head against another opponent. The thrilling battles seen on the animated series can now be recreated on your floor or kitchen table. After reading and familiarizing yourself with these brief steps, you will be ready to go toe-to-toe against even the mighty MegaKabuterimon!

Winning Tips & Techniques

1. Select a Battle Deck of 30 different cards. You can play with decks you and your opponent have already constructed, or you can take turns selecting cards from the Starter Set (two cards will be left over). The Starter Set also includes a Game Mat and two Score Counters to make keeping track of your games a breeze.

Hint: Choose cards that ensure your Rookie Digimon can Digi-volve to Champion, Ultimate and Mega levels. When selecting your cards, start by choosing Mega-level Digimon, and work your way back to its earliest Rookie stages.

2. Place one of the Rookies from your deck face down onto the Duel Zone. Shuffle your deck and deal yourself a 10-card hand. The remaining cards in your deck are placed face down. Both players now flip over their Rookies and the game begins!

3. Determine which Rookie has the power advantage by matching your opponent's Battle Type symbol in the upper-left corner of his or her card with the corresponding symbol in your Digimon Power Box. This will tell you how much power you can use against your opponent. After your opponent does the same, see who unleashed the greater power total.

COLLECTOR'S
VALUE GUIDE™

4. If you have a card that meets the proper requirements, you can now Digi-volve your Rookie by placing the appropriate Champion card on top of it. A coin flip determines who goes first. The second player then has the option of Digi-volving or passing.

Hint: You should choose a Digi-volved character that gives you a Digimon power total higher than your opponent's. But remember, your opponent can turn the tide with a Digi-volve of his or her own!

5. It's now time for everyone's favorite phase – battle! Battle consists of employing Power Option cards with the intention of lowering your opponent's total power while raising your own. Power Option cards are used by each player until they run out of playable cards or voluntarily stop. Once all of the cards have been played, the player with the greater amount of power wins! The victor now consults the score box on his or her card. You win points equal to the level of the Digimon you have defeated. The defeated Digimon are removed, as are all of the Power Option cards.

Hint: The battle types follow a "rock, paper, scissors" approach. Yellow is usually more powerful than green, green is more powerful than red, but red can often defeat yellow.

6. Once the Battle Phase is over, it's time to re-group. Draw enough cards to give yourself a hand of 10 again.

7. If you wish, you can now change your Rookie in the Duel Zone. Play continues as a new battle begins . . .

8. The first player to score 1,000 points wins!

Hint: Defeating powerful Megas and Ultimates will net you more points than beating Rookie and Champion Digimon.

Helpful Battle Card Terms

Battle Deck – The 30 different cards you play against your opponent.

Battle Type – Indicates which Digimon power can be used against your opponent; either ● (red), ■ (green) or ◆ (yellow).

Digi-volve – Raise your Digimon to its next level.

Digi-volve Zone – Spot on Game Mat where you place any card that can Digi-volve your current Digimon.

Duel Zone – Space on Game Mat where your principle cards are turned face up to do battle.

Force FX – Changes the color of your Digimon power.

Online – After selecting a hand of 10 cards, the remaining cards in the deck are placed in the Online space on the Game Mat.

Power – Amount of force you can use against your opponent; determined by opponent's Battle Type.

Power Blast – Card that enhances your battle capabilities.

Rookie – The lowest level of Digimon; followed by Champion, Ultimate and Mega.

MVC: The Most Valuable Cards

Most Valuable Battle Cards

These are the five most valuable battle cards, as determined by their secondary market values. They are all from the set of battle cards numbered St-01 through St-62.

Gatomon™

1st Edition – **$15**

SaberLeomon™

Japanese – **$13**

Boltmon™

1st Edition – **$12**

WereGarurumon™

STS Edition – **$11**

SkullMeramon™

STS Edition – **$10**

Most Valuable Trading Cards

The five most valuable trading cards are all from the highly sought-after first set of American gold cards. "Garurumon™" – $250; "Agumon™" – $225; "Devimon™" – $200; "Izzy & Motimon™" – $190 and "Bakemon™" – $140.

How To Use Your Collector's Value Guide™

1. Locate your card. Cards can be found alphabetically by card name within their corresponding set. The Value Guide begins on page 31 with listings for the Battle Card Starter Set. American cards are pictured on the left, with Japanese cards represented on the right. For each listing you will find the card name, card number and secondary market values. Additionally, holofoil cards are denoted by a "Foil" designation and gold-lettered cards by the word "Gold." These terms appear next to the card to which they refer.

2. Record in the appropriate space the quantity you have of a particular card. Multiply this number by the card's value to determine the "Total Value." Add up all the "Total Value" boxes on each page and record this number in the "Page Totals" box at the bottom of the page.

3. Finish entering your Battle Card totals, and then do the same for your trading cards, beginning with American Trading Cards on page 96. Values for these cards are provided for both the Holofoil and Regular versions of the Unlimited and Exclusive Preview Editions, as well as the extremely rare gold parallel set. Japanese Trading Cards are listed following the American Trading Cards section, and other cards including Card Tactics, Super Bromaido and promotional cards are listed along with their values beginning on page 132. Newer cards may not yet have secondary market value and are either listed as "N/E" (not established) or with a blank line ($___) for you to enter the value.

4. Transfer your completed "Page Totals" to the "Total Value Of My Collection" section beginning on page 138. You will now have a grand total for your Digi-collection!

Battle Card
Starter Set

The American Digi-Battle Starter Set consists of 62 cards numbered St-1 through St-62. The set is available in a now out-of-production 1st Edition as well as an Unlimited edition. Additionally, there are holofoil "chase" Starter Set cards that can be found in booster packs. These extremely rare cards (called "STS" cards) have an "S" at the end of their card numbers.

Within the Starter Set there are 48 American Digi-Battle Character cards, two of which are holofoils, and 14 Power Option cards, one of which is a holofoil.

The Japanese Digital Monster Card Game Starter Set Version 1 is the equivalent to the American Starter Set. These cards are numbered St-1 through St-60 and (with a couple of exceptions) run parallel to the American Starter Set.

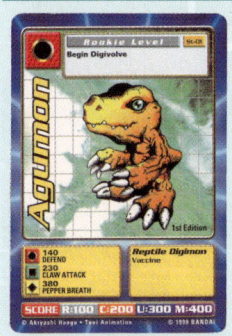

Agumon™ (St-01)

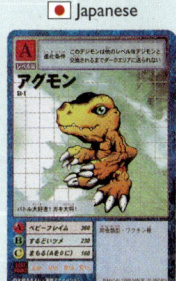

Japanese

	Value	How Many	Total Value
1st Edition	$4.00		
Unlimited	$2.00		
Japanese	$1.25		

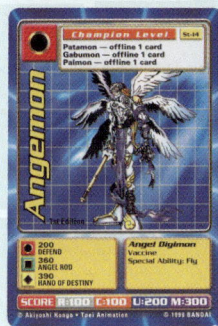

Angemon™ (St-14)

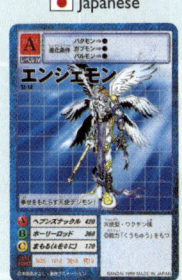

Japanese

	Value	How Many	Total Value
1st Edition	$4.00		
Unlimited	$2.00		
Japanese	$0.75		

Page Totals:	How Many	Total Value

Battle Card Starter Set

Apemon™
(St-43)

 Japanese

	Value	How Many	Total Value
1st Edition	$4.00		
Unlimited	$2.00		
Japanese	$0.50		

Bakemon™
(St-45)

 Japanese

	Value	How Many	Total Value
1st Edition	$3.00		
Unlimited	$1.50		
STS Edition	$7.00		
Japanese	$0.50		

Birdramon™
(St-04)

 Japanese

	Value	How Many	Total Value
1st Edition	$4.00		
Unlimited	$2.00		
Japanese	$0.50		

Biyomon™
(St-03)

Japanese

	Value	How Many	Total Value
1st Edition	$4.00		
Unlimited	$2.00		
Japanese	$0.50		

Page Totals: | How Many | Total Value

COLLECTOR'S VALUE GUIDE™

Blitz™
(St-52)

🔴 Japanese

	Value	How Many	Total Value
1st Edition	$4.00		
Unlimited	$2.00		
Japanese	$0.50		

Candlemon™
(St-41)

🔴 Japanese

	Value	How Many	Total Value
1st Edition	$4.00		
Unlimited	$2.00		
Japanese	$0.50		

Centarumon™
(St-17)

🔴 Japanese

	Value	How Many	Total Value
1st Edition	$4.00		
Unlimited	$2.00		
Japanese	$0.50		

Coelamon™
(St-36)

🔴 Japanese

	Value	How Many	Total Value
1st Edition	$4.00		
Unlimited	$2.00		
STS Edition	$9.00		
Japanese	$0.50		

Battle Card Starter Set

COLLECTOR'S **VALUE GUIDE**™

Page Totals: | How Many | Total Value

Battle Card Starter Set

Counter Attack!™
(St-54)

 Japanese

	Value	How Many	Total Value
1st Edition	$4.00		
Unlimited	$2.00		
Japanese	$0.50		

DemiDevimon™
(St-42)

 Japanese

	Value	How Many	Total Value
1st Edition	$4.00		
Unlimited	$2.00		
Japanese	$0.50		

Digi-Duel™
(St-58)

 Japanese

	Value	How Many	Total Value
1st Edition	$4.00		
Unlimited	$2.00		
Japanese	$0.75		

Digivice Green & Yellow™
(St-60)

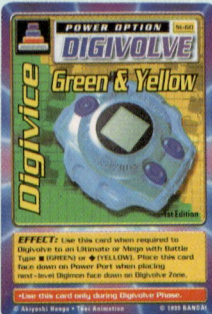

	Value	How Many	Total Value
1st Edition	$4.00		
Unlimited	$2.00		

No Japanese Version

Page Totals: | How Many | Total Value

COLLECTOR'S VALUE GUIDE™

Digivice Red™
(St-59)

	Value	How Many	Total Value
1st Edition	$4.00		
Unlimited	$2.00		

No Japanese Version

Digivice Red & Green™
(St-61)

	Value	How Many	Total Value
1st Edition	$4.00		
Unlimited	$2.00		

No Japanese Version

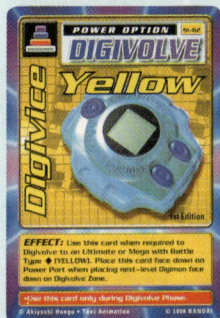

Digivice Yellow™
(St-62)

	Value	How Many	Total Value
1st Edition	$4.00		
Unlimited	$2.00		

No Japanese Version

Dokugumon™
(St-19)

 Japanese

	Value	How Many	Total Value
1st Edition	$4.00		
Unlimited	$2.00		
Japanese	$0.50		

Battle Card Starter Set

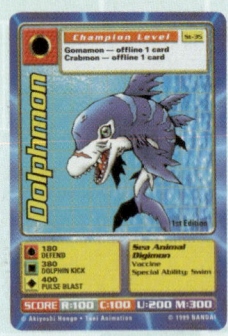

Dolphmon™
(St-35)

 Japanese

	Value	How Many	Total Value
1st Edition	$4.00		
Unlimited	$2.00		
STS Edition	$9.00		
Japanese	$0.50		

Downgrade™
(St-57)

● Japanese

	Value	How Many	Total Value
1st Edition	$3.00		
Unlimited	$1.50		
STS Edition	$5.00		
Japanese	$0.75		

Gabumon™
(St-05)

● Japanese

	Value	How Many	Total Value
1st Edition	$4.00		
Unlimited	$2.00		
Japanese	$0.50		

Garurumon™
(St-06)

● Japanese

	Value	How Many	Total Value
1st Edition	$4.00		
Unlimited	$2.00		
Japanese	$0.50		

Page Totals: How Many / Total Value

COLLECTOR'S VALUE GUIDE™

Gekomon™ (St-27)

🔴 Japanese

	Value	How Many	Total Value
1st Edition	$4.00		
Unlimited	$2.00		
STS Edition	$9.00		
Japanese	$0.50		

Gomamon™ (St-11)

🔴 Japanese

	Value	How Many	Total Value
1st Edition	$4.00		
Unlimited	$2.00		
Japanese	$1.25		

Gotsumon™ (St-23)

🔴 Japanese

	Value	How Many	Total Value
1st Edition	$4.00		
Unlimited	$2.00		
Japanese	$0.50		

Green Offensive™ (St-51)

No Japanese Version

	Value	How Many	Total Value
1st Edition	$4.00		
Unlimited	$2.00		

Battle Card Starter Set

COLLECTOR'S VALUE GUIDE™

Page Totals: | How Many | Total Value

Battle Card Starter Set

Greymon™ (St-02)

● Japanese

	Value	How Many	Total Value
1st Edition	$4.00		
Unlimited	$2.00		
Japanese	$1.25		

Hercules-Kabuterimon™ (St-33)

● Japanese

Foil — Foil

	Value	How Many	Total Value
1st Edition	$10.00		
Unlimited	$6.00		
Japanese	$0.50		

Ikkakumon™ (St-12)

● Japanese

	Value	How Many	Total Value
1st Edition	$4.00		
Unlimited	$2.00		
Japanese	$0.50		

Kabuterimon™ (St-08)

● Japanese

	Value	How Many	Total Value
1st Edition	$4.00		
Unlimited	$2.00		
Japanese	$0.50		

Page Totals: How Many / Total Value

COLLECTOR'S VALUE GUIDE™

Kimeramon™
(St-21)

🔴 Japanese

Gold

	Value	How Many	Total Value
1st Edition	$4.00		
Unlimited	$2.00		
Japanese	$0.50		

Kunemon™
(St-18)

🔴 Japanese

	Value	How Many	Total Value
1st Edition	$5.00		
Unlimited	$3.00		
Japanese	$0.50		

Mammothmon™
(St-46)

🔴 Japanese

	Value	How Many	Total Value
1st Edition	$5.00		
Unlimited	$3.00		
STS Edition	$10.00		
Japanese	$0.50		

MarineDevimon™
(St-39)

🔴 Japanese

	Value	How Many	Total Value
1st Edition	$4.00		
Unlimited	$2.00		
Japanese	$0.50		

COLLECTOR'S VALUE GUIDE™

Page Totals: | How Many | Total Value

Battle Card Starter Set

Battle Card Starter Set

MegaKabuterimon™
(St-28)

🔴 Japanese

	Value	How Many	Total Value
1st Edition	$4.00		
Unlimited	$2.00		
STS Edition	$9.00		
Japanese	$0.50		

Metal Attack™
(St-53)

🔴 Japanese

	Value	How Many	Total Value
1st Edition	$4.00		
Unlimited	$2.00		
STS Edition	$9.00		
Japanese	$0.50		

Musyamon™
(St-20)

🔴 Japanese

	Value	How Many	Total Value
1st Edition	$4.00		
Unlimited	$2.00		
Japanese	$0.50		

Nanimon™
(St-15)

🔴 Japanese

	Value	How Many	Total Value
1st Edition	$4.00		
Unlimited	$2.00		
Japanese	$0.50		

Page Totals: | How Many | Total Value |

COLLECTOR'S VALUE GUIDE™

Battle Card Starter Set

Octomon™ (St-37)

● Japanese

	Value	How Many	Total Value
1st Edition	$4.00		
Unlimited	$2.00		
STS Edition	$9.00		
Japanese	$0.50		

Okuwamon™ (St-31)

● Japanese

	Value	How Many	Total Value
1st Edition	$5.00		
Unlimited	$3.00		
STS Edition	$10.00		
Japanese	$0.75		

Otamamon™ (St-24)

● Japanese

	Value	How Many	Total Value
1st Edition	$4.00		
Unlimited	$2.00		
Japanese	$0.50		

Palmon™ (St-09)

● Japanese

	Value	How Many	Total Value
1st Edition	$4.00		
Unlimited	$2.00		
Japanese	$0.75		

COLLECTOR'S VALUE GUIDE™

Page Totals: | How Many | Total Value

Battle Card Starter Set

Patamon™ (St-13)

● Japanese

	Value	How Many	Total Value
1st Edition	$4.00		
Unlimited	$2.00		
Japanese	$0.50		

Piximon™ (St-30)

● Japanese

	Value	How Many	Total Value
1st Edition	$5.00		
Unlimited	$3.00		
STS Edition	$10.00		
Japanese	$0.75		

Plug-In Attack A™ (St-49)

● Japanese

No American Version

	Value	How Many	Total Value
Japanese	$0.35		

Plug-In B™ (St-51)

● Japanese

No American Version

	Value	How Many	Total Value
Japanese	$0.35		

Page Totals: | How Many | Total Value |

COLLECTOR'S VALUE GUIDE

Plug-In Defense C™
(St-50)

No American Version

● Japanese

	Value	How Many	Total Value
Japanese	$0.50		

Pukumon™
(St-40)

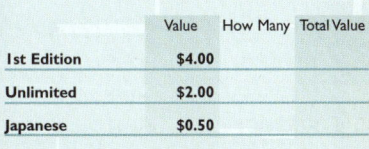

Foil

● Japanese

	Value	How Many	Total Value
1st Edition	$4.00		
Unlimited	$2.00		
Japanese	$0.50		

Red Offensive™
(St-49)

	Value	How Many	Total Value
1st Edition	$4.00		
Unlimited	$2.00		

No Japanese Version

Rockmon™
(St-22)

● Japanese

	Value	How Many	Total Value
1st Edition	$4.00		
Unlimited	$2.00		
Japanese	$0.50		

Battle Card Starter Set

COLLECTOR'S VALUE GUIDE™

Page Totals: | How Many | Total Value

Battle Card Starter Set

SaberLeomon™ (St-34)

Foil   *Gold*

● Japanese

	Value	How Many	Total Value
1st Edition	$4.00		
Unlimited	$2.00		
Japanese	$12.00		

SkullGreymon™ (St-32)

● Japanese

	Value	How Many	Total Value
1st Edition	$5.50		
Unlimited	$3.25		
STS Edition	$10.00		
Japanese	$0.50		

SkullMeramon™ (St-48)

● Japanese

	Value	How Many	Total Value
1st Edition	$5.50		
Unlimited	$3.25		
STS Edition	$10.00		
Japanese	$0.50		

Starmon™ (St-26)

● Japanese

	Value	How Many	Total Value
1st Edition	$4.00		
Unlimited	$2.00		
STS Edition	$9.00		
Japanese	$0.50		

Page Totals:

COLLECTOR'S VALUE GUIDE™

Tentomon™ (St-07)

● Japanese

	Value	How Many	Total Value
1st Edition	$4.00		
Unlimited	$2.00		
Japanese	$0.50		

To Champion™ (St-55)

● Japanese

	Value	How Many	Total Value
1st Edition	$4.00		
Unlimited	$2.00		
Japanese	$0.50		

Togemon™ (St-10)

● Japanese

	Value	How Many	Total Value
1st Edition	$4.00		
Unlimited	$2.00		
Japanese	$0.50		

Tortomon™ (St-25)

● Japanese

	Value	How Many	Total Value
1st Edition	$4.00		
Unlimited	$2.00		
STS Edition	$9.00		
Japanese	$0.50		

COLLECTOR'S VALUE GUIDE™

Page Totals: | How Many | Total Value

Battle Card Starter Set

45

Battle Card Starter Set

Triceramon™
(St-29)

Japanese

	Value	How Many	Total Value
1st Edition	$4.00		
Unlimited	$2.00		
STS Edition	$9.00		
Japanese	$0.50		

Ultra Digivolve™
(St-56)

Japanese

Foil   Foil

	Value	How Many	Total Value
1st Edition	$6.00		
Unlimited	$3.00		
Japanese	$6.00		

Unimon™
(St-16)

Japanese

	Value	How Many	Total Value
1st Edition	$4.00		
Unlimited	$2.00		
Japanese	$0.50		

WereGarurumon™
(St-47)

Japanese

Gold

	Value	How Many	Total Value
1st Edition	$7.00		
Unlimited	$4.00		
STS Edition	$11.00		
Japanese	$0.50		

Page Totals: | How Many | Total Value

COLLECTOR'S VALUE GUIDE™

Winning Percentage 40%!™
(St-59)

No American Version

🔴 Japanese

	Value	How Many	Total Value
Japanese	$0.50		

Winning Percentage 60%!™
(St-60)

No American Version

🔴 Japanese

	Value	How Many	Total Value
Japanese	$0.50		

Wizardmon™
(St-44)

🔴 Japanese

	Value	How Many	Total Value
1st Edition	$9.00		
Unlimited	$6.00		
Japanese	$1.00		

Yellow Offensive™
(St-50)

	Value	How Many	Total Value
1st Edition	$4.00		
Unlimited	$2.00		

No Japanese Version

COLLECTOR'S VALUE GUIDE™

Page Totals: | How Many | Total Value

Battle Card Starter Set

47

Zudomon™
(St-38)

🔴 Japanese

	Value	How Many	Total Value
1st Edition	$4.00		
Unlimited	$2.00		
Japanese	$0.50		

Battle Card Starter Set

Page Totals: | How Many | Total Value

COLLECTOR'S VALUE GUIDE™

Battle Card
Starter Set Version 2

Battle Card Starter Set Version 2 has no equivalent American cards. You can tell a Version 2 pack of cards because they are sold in red-colored packages of 32 cards. Sixty cards were released in the set, but 9 of them are duplicates of cards found in the first Starter Set of Japanese cards. Secondary market values have not yet been established for these cards, so we have left a blank line for you to write in the values once they do become available.

Value
$_____

How Many

Total Value

Andromon™ (St-78)

Value
$_____

How Many

Total Value

Angemon™ (St-67)

Value
$_____

How Many

Total Value

Angewomon™ (St-77)

Value
$_____

How Many

Total Value

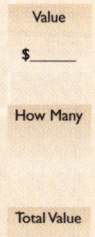

AtolaKabuterimon™ (St-98)

COLLECTOR'S VALUE GUIDE™

Page Totals: | How Many | Total Value

49

Battle Card Starter Set Version 2

Battle Card Starter Set Version 2

Bad Monzaemon™ (St-83)

Value
$_____

How Many

Total Value

Big Mamemon™ (St-93)

Value
$_____

How Many

Total Value

Birdramon™ (St-85)

Value
$_____

How Many

Total Value

Burumeramon™ (St-96)

Value
$_____

How Many

Total Value

Centarumon™ (St-75)

Value
$_____

How Many

Total Value

Counter-Attack!™ (St-105)

Value
$_____

How Many

Total Value

Page Totals:	How Many	Total Value

COLLECTOR'S VALUE GUIDE™

Devimon™ (St-76)

Value
$_____

How Many

Total Value

Dolphmon™ (St-68)

Value
$_____

How Many

Total Value

Drag Into Water!™
(St-110)

Value
$_____

How Many

Total Value

Garurumon™ (St-88)

Value
$_____

How Many

Total Value

Gotsumon™ (St-62)

Value
$_____

How Many

Total Value

Greymon™ (St-91)

Value
$_____

How Many

Total Value

Gold

Battle Card Starter Set Version 2

COLLECTOR'S VALUE GUIDE™

Page Totals:	How Many	Total Value

51

Battle Card Starter Set Version 2

Hagurumon™ (St-64)

Value $_____
How Many
Total Value

Hangyomon™ (St-82)

Value $_____
How Many
Total Value

I Can't Lose Like This!™ (St-109)

Value $_____
How Many
Total Value

I Feel Hurt™ (St-103)

Value $_____
How Many
Total Value

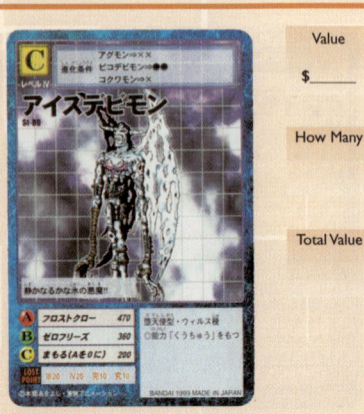

IceDevimon™ (St-80)

Value $_____
How Many
Total Value

It Is Great To Be Able To Fly!™ (St-108)

Value $_____
How Many
Total Value

Page Totals: How Many ___ Total Value ___

COLLECTOR'S VALUE GUIDE™

52

Kabuterimon™ (St-66)   Value $____   How Many   Total Value

Kamenolimon™ (St-86)   Value $____   How Many   Total Value

Kokuwamon™ (St-65)   Value $____   How Many   Total Value

Kunemon™ (St-63)   Value $____   How Many   Total Value

Kuwagamon™ (St-73)   Value $____   How Many   Total Value

Leomon™ (St-72)   Value $____   How Many   Total Value

Battle Card Starter Set Version 2

COLLECTOR'S VALUE GUIDE™

Page Totals:	How Many	Total Value

53

Battle Card Starter Set Version 2

Libolumon™ (St-84)

Value $_____

How Many _____

Total Value _____

Megadramon™ (St-94)

Value $_____

How Many _____

Total Value _____

Gold

Mojymon™ (St-90)

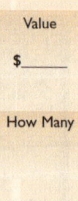

Value $_____

How Many _____

Total Value _____

Ogremon™ (St-89)

Value $_____

How Many _____

Total Value _____

Ohkuwamon™ (St-79)

Value $_____

How Many _____

Total Value _____

Palmon™ (St-111)

Value $_____

How Many _____

Total Value _____

Page Totals:	How Many	Total Value

COLLECTOR'S VALUE GUIDE™

54

Battle Card Starter Set Version 2

Panjamon™ (St-95)

Value
$_____

How Many

Total Value

Plug-In S™ (St-100)

Value
$_____

How Many

Total Value

Preshiomon™ (St-87)

Value
$_____

How Many

Total Value

A Rival Is Vaccine!™ (St-107)

Value
$_____

How Many

Total Value

SkullMeramon™ (St-71)

Value
$_____

How Many

Total Value

Tankmon™ (St-81)

Value
$_____

How Many

Total Value

COLLECTOR'S
VALUE GUIDE™

Page Totals:	How Many	Total Value

Battle Card Starter Set Version 2

This Is A Return Match!™ (St-104)

Value $_____
How Many
Total Value
Foil

Training Manual™ (St-99)

Value $_____
How Many
Total Value

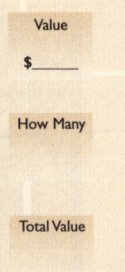

Unimon™ (St-74)

Value $_____
How Many
Total Value

VenomMyotismon™ (St-97)

Value $_____
How Many
Total Value
Foil

WarGreymon™ (St-61)

Value $_____
How Many
Total Value
Foil

Whamon™ (St-92)

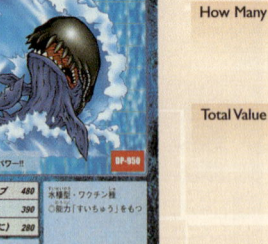

Value $_____
How Many
Total Value

Page Totals: How Many _____ Total Value _____

COLLECTOR'S VALUE GUIDE™

56

Battle Card Starter Set Version 2

Winning Percentage 40%!™ (St-101)

Value $_____
How Many
Total Value

Winning Percentage 60%!™ (St-102)

Value $_____
How Many
Total Value

Wizardmon™ (St-70)

Value $_____
How Many
Total Value

Zudomon™ (St-69)

Value $_____
How Many
Total Value

Page Totals:	How Many	Total Value

COLLECTOR'S VALUE GUIDE™

Booster Card
Series 1 & 2

Booster cards for the Japanese Starter Sets have been available in Japan for some time now. In the United States, Upper Deck released the 54-card Booster Card Series 1 in March 2000. Series 2 followed with another 54 cards in May, and Series 3 is set for a late-summer release.

AeroVeedramon™ (Bo-88)

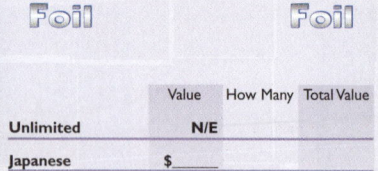

Foil — Foil — ● Japanese

	Value	How Many	Total Value
Unlimited	N/E		
Japanese	$		

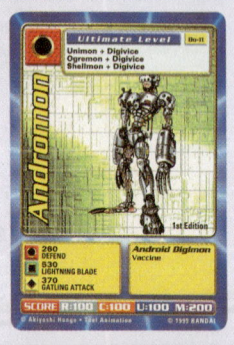

Andromon™ (Bo-11)

● Japanese

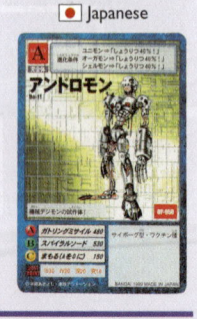

	Value	How Many	Total Value
1st Edition	$4.00		
Unlimited	$2.00		
Japanese	$		

Angewomon™ (Bo-16)

● Japanese

	Value	How Many	Total Value
1st Edition	$6.50		
Unlimited	$2.75		
Japanese	$		

Page Totals:	How Many	Total Value

COLLECTOR'S VALUE GUIDE™

Aquatic Attack™ (Bo-45)

● Japanese

	Value	How Many	Total Value
1st Edition	$1.00		
Unlimited	$0.65		
Japanese	$_____		

Asuramon™ (Bo-24)

● Japanese

	Value	How Many	Total Value
1st Edition	$3.50		
Unlimited	$1.50		
Japanese	$_____		

Black Gears™ (Bo-104) U.S. (Bo-103) Japanese

● Japanese

	Value	How Many	Total Value
Unlimited	N/E		
Japanese	$_____		

Blossomon™ (Bo-90)

● Japanese

	Value	How Many	Total Value
Unlimited	N/E		
Japanese	$_____		

Booster Card Series 1 & 2

COLLECTOR'S VALUE GUIDE™

Page Totals: | How Many | Total Value

59

Booster Card Series 1 & 2

Boltmon™ (Bo-41)

Gold

🔴 Japanese

	Value	How Many	Total Value
1st Edition	$12.00		
Unlimited	$6.00		
Japanese	$		

Bomb Dive™ (Bo-52)

🔴 Japanese

	Value	How Many	Total Value
1st Edition	$4.00		
Unlimited	$2.00		
Japanese	$		

Cherrymon™ (Bo-92)

🔴 Japanese

	Value	How Many	Total Value
Unlimited	N/E		
Japanese	$		

Coral Rip™ (Bo-44)

🔴 Japanese

	Value	How Many	Total Value
1st Edition	$1.00		
Unlimited	$0.65		
Japanese	$		

Page Totals:	How Many	Total Value

COLLECTOR'S VALUE GUIDE™

Booster Card Series 1 & 2

Crabmon™
(Bo-28)

● Japanese

	Value	How Many	Total Value
1st Edition	$2.00		
Unlimited	$1.00		
Japanese	$_____		

Crest of Courage™
(Bo-100) U.S.
(Bo-99) Japanese

● Japanese

	Value	How Many	Total Value
Unlimited	N/E		
Japanese	$_____		

Crest of Friendship™
(Bo-103) U.S.
(Bo-102) Japanese

● Japanese

	Value	How Many	Total Value
Unlimited	N/E		
Japanese	$_____		

Crest of Reliability™
(Bo-101) U.S.
(Bo-100) Japanese

● Japanese

	Value	How Many	Total Value
Unlimited	N/E		
Japanese	$_____		

COLLECTOR'S VALUE GUIDE™

Page Totals: | How Many | Total Value

Booster Card Series 1 & 2

Crest of Sincerity™
(Bo-102) U.S.
(Bo-101) Japanese

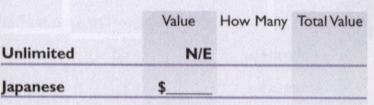

● Japanese

	Value	How Many	Total Value
Unlimited	N/E		
Japanese	$		

Crest Tag™
(Bo-99) U.S.
(Bo-98) Japanese

● Japanese

	Value	How Many	Total Value
Unlimited	N/E		
Japanese	$		

Cyclonemon™
(Bo-78)

● Japanese

	Value	How Many	Total Value
Unlimited	N/E		
Japanese	$		

DarkTyrannomon™
(Bo-79)

● Japanese

	Value	How Many	Total Value
Unlimited	N/E		
Japanese	$		

Page Totals: | How Many | Total Value

COLLECTOR'S VALUE GUIDE™

62

Datamon™ (Bo-67)

● Japanese

	Value	How Many	Total Value
Unlimited	N/E		
Japanese	$____		

Deltamon™ (Bo-74)

● Japanese

	Value	How Many	Total Value
Unlimited	N/E		
Japanese	$____		

Depth Charge™ (Bo-54)

● Japanese

	Value	How Many	Total Value
1st Edition	$2.00		
Unlimited	$1.00		
Japanese	$____		

Deramon™ (Bo-91)

● Japanese

	Value	How Many	Total Value
Unlimited	N/E		
Japanese	$____		

COLLECTOR'S VALUE GUIDE™

Page Totals: | How Many | Total Value

Booster Card Series 1 & 2

63

Booster Card Series 1 & 2

Devimon™ (Bo-02)

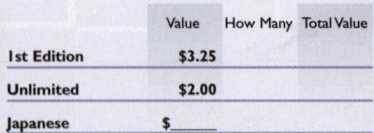

Foil

● Japanese

	Value	How Many	Total Value
1st Edition	$3.25		
Unlimited	$2.00		
Japanese	$_____		

Digiruption™ (Bo-53)

● Japanese

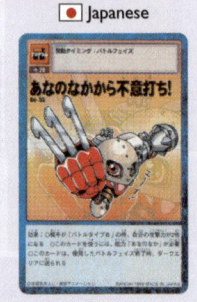

	Value	How Many	Total Value
1st Edition	$3.50		
Unlimited	$1.50		
Japanese	$_____		

Digitamamon™ (Bo-70)

● Japanese

	Value	How Many	Total Value
Unlimited	N/E		
Japanese	$_____		

Dragomon™ (Bo-33)

● Japanese

	Value	How Many	Total Value
1st Edition	$2.00		
Unlimited	$1.00		
Japanese	$_____		

Page Totals: | How Many | Total Value

COLLECTOR'S VALUE GUIDE™

Drimogemon™ (Bo-10)

● Japanese

	Value	How Many	Total Value
1st Edition	$2.00		
Unlimited	$1.00		
Japanese	$____		

Ebidramon™ (Bo-18)

● Japanese

	Value	How Many	Total Value
1st Edition	$2.50		
Unlimited	$1.25		
Japanese	$____		

Elecmon™ (Bo-61)

● Japanese

	Value	How Many	Total Value
Unlimited	N/E		
Japanese	$____		

Etemon™ (Bo-57)

● Japanese

	Value	How Many	Total Value
Unlimited	N/E		
Japanese	$____		

Booster Cards Series 1 & 2

COLLECTOR'S VALUE GUIDE™

Page Totals: | How Many | Total Value

65

Booster Cards Series 1 & 2

Even Steven™ (Bo-51)

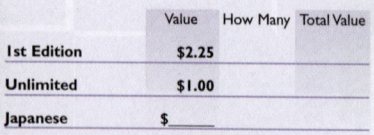

🔴 Japanese

	Value	How Many	Total Value
1st Edition	$2.25		
Unlimited	$1.00		
Japanese	$_____		

ExTyrannomon™ (Bo-73)

🔴 Japanese

	Value	How Many	Total Value
Unlimited	N/E		
Japanese	$_____		

Flood™ (Bo-105)

No Japanese Version

	Value	How Many	Total Value
Unlimited	$_____		

Floramon™ (Bo-81)

🔴 Japanese

	Value	How Many	Total Value
Unlimited	N/E		
Japanese	$_____		

Page Totals: How Many ___ Total Value ___

COLLECTOR'S VALUE GUIDE™

Fly Away™ (Bo-46)

● Japanese

	Value	How Many	Total Value
1st Edition	$1.00		
Unlimited	$0.65		
Japanese	$		

Fly-Trap™ (Bo-43)

● Japanese

	Value	How Many	Total Value
1st Edition	$1.00		
Unlimited	$0.65		
Japanese	$		

Frigimon™ (Bo-07)

● Japanese

	Value	How Many	Total Value
1st Edition	$2.00		
Unlimited	$1.00		
Japanese	$		

Garbagemon™ (Bo-93)

● Japanese

	Value	How Many	Total Value
Unlimited	N/E		
Japanese	$		

COLLECTOR'S VALUE GUIDE™

Page Totals: | How Many | Total Value

Booster Cards Series 1 & 2

67

Booster Cards Series 1 & 2

Garudamon™ (Bo-89)

Japanese

	Value	How Many	Total Value
Unlimited	N/E		
Japanese	$_____		

Gatomon™ (Bo-15)

Gold   Gold

Japanese

	Value	How Many	Total Value
1st Edition	$15.00		
Unlimited	$7.00		
Japanese	$_____		

Gatomon™ (Bo-77)

Gold   Gold

Japanese

	Value	How Many	Total Value
Unlimited	N/E		
Japanese	$_____		

Gazimon™ (Bo-60)

Japanese

	Value	How Many	Total Value
Unlimited	N/E		
Japanese	$_____		

Page Totals: | How Many | Total Value

COLLECTOR'S VALUE GUIDE™

Gesomon™ (Bo-30)

◉ Japanese

	Value	How Many	Total Value
1st Edition	$2.00		
Unlimited	$1.00		
Japanese	$_____		

Giromon™ (Bo-68)

◉ Japanese

	Value	How Many	Total Value
Unlimited	N/E		
Japanese	$_____		

Gizamon™ (Bo-71)

◉ Japanese

	Value	How Many	Total Value
Unlimited	N/E		
Japanese	$_____		

Gorillamon™ (Bo-19)

◉ Japanese

	Value	How Many	Total Value
1st Edition	$2.00		
Unlimited	$1.00		
Japanese	$_____		

Booster Cards Series 1 & 2

COLLECTOR'S VALUE GUIDE™

Page Totals: | How Many | Total Value

69

Booster Cards Series 1 & 2

Green Digivice™ (Bo-97)

◉ Japanese

	Value	How Many	Total Value
Unlimited	N/E		
Japanese	$_____		

Gryphonmon™ (Bo-95)

◉ Japanese

	Value	How Many	Total Value
Unlimited	N/E		
Japanese	$_____		

Iron Drill™ (Bo-47)

◉ Japanese

	Value	How Many	Total Value
1st Edition	$1.00		
Unlimited	$0.65		
Japanese	$_____		

Jagamon™ (Bo-26)

◉ Japanese

	Value	How Many	Total Value
1st Edition	$2.00		
Unlimited	$1.00		
Japanese	$_____		

Page Totals: How Many / Total Value

COLLECTOR'S VALUE GUIDE™

70

Booster Cards Series 1 & 2

Kiwimon™ (Bo-85)

🔴 Japanese

	Value	How Many	Total Value
Unlimited	N/E		
Japanese	$		

Kokatorimon™ (Bo-56)

🔴 Japanese

	Value	How Many	Total Value
Unlimited	N/E		
Japanese	$		

Kuwagamon™ (Bo-13)

🔴 Japanese

	Value	How Many	Total Value
1st Edition	$2.25		
Unlimited	$1.00		
Japanese	$		

LadyDevimon™ (Bo-22)

Gold

	Value	How Many	Total Value
1st Edition	$3.50		
Unlimited	$1.50		
Japanese	$		

COLLECTOR'S VALUE GUIDE™

Page Totals:	How Many	Total Value

Booster Cards Series 1 & 2

Leomon™
(Bo-03)

Gold

● Japanese

	Value	How Many	Total Value
1st Edition	$4.00		
Unlimited	$2.00		
Japanese	$_____		

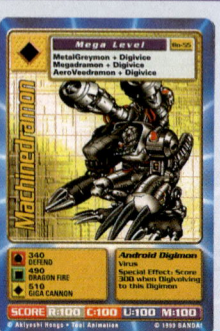

Machinedramon™
(Bo-55)

Foil   **Foil**

● Japanese

	Value	How Many	Total Value
Unlimited	N/E		
Japanese	$_____		

Magnadramon™
(Bo-17)

● Japanese

	Value	How Many	Total Value
1st Edition	$5.00		
Unlimited	$2.25		
Japanese	$_____		

Mamemon™
(Bo-64)

● Japanese

	Value	How Many	Total Value
Unlimited	N/E		
Japanese	$_____		

Page Totals: | How Many | Total Value |

COLLECTOR'S VALUE GUIDE™

MarineAngemon™ (Bo-34)

Gold

● Japanese

	Value	How Many	Total Value
1st Edition	$8.00		
Unlimited	$4.00		
Japanese	$_____		

Meat™ (Bo-106)

● Japanese

	Value	How Many	Total Value
Unlimited	N/E		
Japanese	$_____		

Megadramon™ (Bo-69)

● Japanese

	Value	How Many	Total Value
Unlimited	N/E		
Japanese	$_____		

MegaSeadramon™ (Bo-31)

● Japanese

	Value	How Many	Total Value
1st Edition	$3.00		
Unlimited	$1.25		
Japanese	$_____		

COLLECTOR'S VALUE GUIDE™

Page Totals: | How Many | Total Value

Booster Cards Series 1 & 2

73

Booster Cards Series 1 & 2

Meramon™ (Bo-05)

● Japanese

	Value	How Many	Total Value
1st Edition	$4.50		
Unlimited	$2.25		
Japanese	$_____		

MetalEtemon™ (Bo-27)

● Japanese

Foil

	Value	How Many	Total Value
1st Edition	$5.00		
Unlimited	$2.25		
Japanese	$_____		

MetalGreymon™ (Bo-01)

● Japanese

PHOTO UNAVAILABLE

	Value	How Many	Total Value
1st Edition	$5.00		
Unlimited	$2.25		
Japanese	$_____		

MetalGreymon™ (Bo-80)

● Japanese

Gold   *Foil*

	Value	How Many	Total Value
Unlimited	N/E		
Japanese	$_____		

Page Totals: | How Many | Total Value |

COLLECTOR'S VALUE GUIDE™

74

MetalMamemon™ (Bo-65)

● Japanese

	Value	How Many	Total Value
Unlimited	N/E		
Japanese	$		

MetalSeadramon™ (Bo-35)

● Japanese

Foil

	Value	How Many	Total Value
1st Edition	$6.50		
Unlimited	$2.75		
Japanese	$		

Minotarumon™ (Bo-21)

● Japanese

	Value	How Many	Total Value
1st Edition	$2.00		
Unlimited	$1.00		
Japanese	$		

Mojyamon™ (Bo-14)

● Japanese

	Value	How Many	Total Value
1st Edition	$2.00		
Unlimited	$1.00		
Japanese	$		

COLLECTOR'S VALUE GUIDE™

Page Totals: | How Many | Total Value

Booster Cards Series 1 & 2

Booster Cards Series 1 & 2

Monochromon™ (Bo-12)

• Japanese

	Value	How Many	Total Value
1st Edition	$2.00		
Unlimited	$1.00		
Japanese	$____		

Monzaemon™ (Bo-62)

• Japanese

	Value	How Many	Total Value
Unlimited	N/E		
Japanese	$____		

Mushroomon™ (Bo-82)

• Japanese

	Value	How Many	Total Value
Unlimited	N/E		
Japanese	$____		

Myotismon™ (Bo-38)

• Japanese

	Value	How Many	Total Value
1st Edition	$3.00		
Unlimited	$1.50		
Japanese	$____		

Page Totals: How Many | Total Value

COLLECTOR'S VALUE GUIDE™

Myotismon™ (Bo-76)

Gold   Gold

🔴 Japanese

	Value	How Many	Total Value
Unlimited	N/E		
Japanese	$_____		

Numemon™ (Bo-63)

🔴 Japanese

	Value	How Many	Total Value
Unlimited	N/E		
Japanese	$_____		

Ogremon™ (Bo-04)

🔴 Japanese

	Value	How Many	Total Value
1st Edition	$2.00		
Unlimited	$1.00		
Japanese	$_____		

Option Eater™ (Bo-49)

🔴 Japanese

	Value	How Many	Total Value
1st Edition	$1.00		
Unlimited	$0.65		
Japanese	$_____		

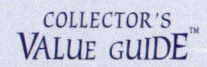

COLLECTOR'S VALUE GUIDE™

Page Totals: | How Many | Total Value

Organic Enhancer™
(Bo-48)

🔴 Japanese

	Value	How Many	Total Value
1st Edition	$1.00		
Unlimited	$0.65		
Japanese	$_____		

Phantomon™
(Bo-39)

🔴 Japanese

	Value	How Many	Total Value
1st Edition	$2.00		
Unlimited	$1.00		
Japanese	$_____		

Phoenixmon™
(Bo-94)

🔴 Japanese

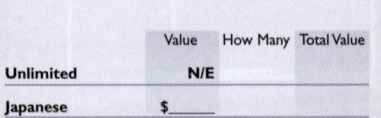

Gold

	Value	How Many	Total Value
Unlimited	N/E		
Japanese	$_____		

Piedmon™
(Bo-42)

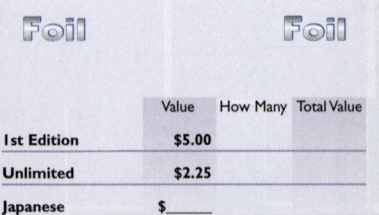

🔴 Japanese

Foil   Foil

	Value	How Many	Total Value
1st Edition	$5.00		
Unlimited	$2.25		
Japanese	$_____		

Page Totals: | How Many | Total Value

COLLECTOR'S VALUE GUIDE™

Pluck™ (Bo-108)

• Japanese

	Value	How Many	Total Value
Unlimited	N/E		
Japanese	$		

Power Freeze™ (Bo-50)

• Japanese

	Value	How Many	Total Value
1st Edition	$1.00		
Unlimited	$0.65		
Japanese	$		

Pumpkinmon™ (Bo-37)

• Japanese

	Value	How Many	Total Value
1st Edition	$2.50		
Unlimited	$1.00		
Japanese	$		

Puppetmon™ (Bo-96)

• Japanese

Foil

	Value	How Many	Total Value
Unlimited	N/E		
Japanese	$		

COLLECTOR'S VALUE GUIDE™

Page Totals: | How Many | Total Value

Booster Cards Series 1 & 2

Booster Cards Series 1 & 2

Raremon™ (Bo-72)

◉ Japanese

	Value	How Many	Total Value
Unlimited	N/E		
Japanese	$		

Red & Yellow Digivice™ (Bo-98)

No Japanese Version

	Value	How Many	Total Value
Unlimited	$		

RedVegiemon™ (Bo-87)

◉ Japanese

	Value	How Many	Total Value
Unlimited	N/E		
Japanese	$		

Roachmon™ (Bo-23)

◉ Japanese

	Value	How Many	Total Value
1st Edition	$2.00		
Unlimited	$1.00		
Japanese	$		

Page Totals:

COLLECTOR'S VALUE GUIDE™

Scorpiomon™
(Bo-32)

● Japanese

	Value	How Many	Total Value
1st Edition	$2.00		
Unlimited	$1.00		
Japanese	$_____		

Seadramon™
(Bo-06)

● Japanese

	Value	How Many	Total Value
1st Edition	$2.00		
Unlimited	$1.00		
Japanese	$_____		

Shellmon™
(Bo-09)

● Japanese

	Value	How Many	Total Value
1st Edition	$2.00		
Unlimited	$1.00		
Japanese	$_____		

ShogunGekomon™
(Bo-08)

● Japanese

	Value	How Many	Total Value
1st Edition	$2.00		
Unlimited	$1.00		
Japanese	$_____		

Booster Card Series 1 & 2

COLLECTOR'S VALUE GUIDE™

Page Totals: | How Many | Total Value

Booster Card Series 1 & 2

SkullMammothmon™ (Bo-40)

🔴 Japanese

	Value	How Many	Total Value
1st Edition	$5.00		
Unlimited	$2.25		
Japanese	$_____		

Snimon™ (Bo-25)

🔴 Japanese

	Value	How Many	Total Value
1st Edition	$2.00		
Unlimited	$1.00		
Japanese	$_____		

Sukamon™ (Bo-59)

🔴 Japanese

	Value	How Many	Total Value
Unlimited	N/E		
Japanese	$_____		

Syakomon™ (Bo-29)

🔴 Japanese

	Value	How Many	Total Value
1st Edition	$1.00		
Unlimited	$0.65		
Japanese	$_____		

Page Totals: | How Many | Total Value

COLLECTOR'S VALUE GUIDE™

Tapirmon™ (Bo-36)

● Japanese

	Value	How Many	Total Value
1st Edition	$2.00		
Unlimited	$1.00		
Japanese	$_____		

Togemon™ (Bo-84)

● Japanese

	Value	How Many	Total Value
Unlimited	N/E		
Japanese	$_____		

Tuskmon™ (Bo-75)

● Japanese

	Value	How Many	Total Value
Unlimited	N/E		
Japanese	$_____		

Tyrannomon™ (Bo-66)

● Japanese

	Value	How Many	Total Value
Unlimited	N/E		
Japanese	$_____		

COLLECTOR'S VALUE GUIDE™

Page Totals: | How Many | Total Value

Booster Card Series 1 & 2

83

Veedramon™
(Bo-83)

🔴 Japanese

	Value	How Many	Total Value
Unlimited	N/E		
Japanese	$		

Vilemon™
(Bo-20)

🔴 Japanese

	Value	How Many	Total Value
1st Edition	$2.00		
Unlimited	$1.00		
Japanese	$		

Waterproof™
(Bo-107)

🔴 Japanese

	Value	How Many	Total Value
Unlimited	N/E		
Japanese	$		

Whamon™
(Bo-58)

🔴 Japanese

	Value	How Many	Total Value
Unlimited	N/E		
Japanese	$		

Page Totals: How Many | Total Value

Booster Card Series 1 & 2

COLLECTOR'S VALUE GUIDE™

Winning Percentage 40%!™
(Bo-104)

● Japanese

No American Version

	Value	How Many	Total Value
Japanese	$		

Winning Percentage 60%!™
(Bo-105)

● Japanese

No American Version

	Value	How Many	Total Value
Japanese	$		

Woodmon™
(Bo-86)

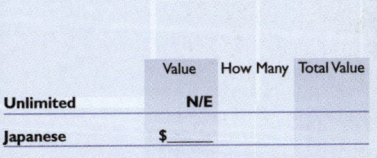

● Japanese

	Value	How Many	Total Value
Unlimited	N/E		
Japanese	$		

Booster Card Series 1 & 2

COLLECTOR'S VALUE GUIDE™

Page Totals:	How Many	Total Value

85

Booster Card Series 3

Although the Japanese version has been available for some time, Booster Set Series 3 has not yet been released in the United States. The U.S. version is set to be released in late summer 2000 and is expected to parallel the Japanese set. These cards are numbered Bo-109 through Bo-162 and picture many Digimon never before seen on any other card to date. Secondary market values have not yet been established for these cards, so we have left a blank line for you to write in the values once they do become available.

Aim For The Strongest Evolution!™ (Bo-157)

Value $_____

How Many

Total Value

Airdramon™ (Bo-131)

Value $_____

How Many

Total Value

Alulamon™ (Bo-127)

Value $_____

How Many

Total Value

Babamon™ (Bo-146)

Value $_____

How Many

Total Value

Page Totals: | How Many | Total Value

Booster Card Series 3

Bad Seadramon™ (Bo-143)

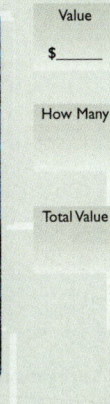

Value $_____

How Many

Total Value

Betamon™ (Bo-111)

Value $_____

How Many

Total Value

Clockmon™ (Bo-112)

Value $_____

How Many

Total Value

Crest Of Hope™ (Bo-148)

Value $_____

How Many

Total Value

Crest Of Knowledge™ (Bo-147)

Value $_____

How Many

Total Value

Crest Of Love™ (Bo-149)

Value $_____

How Many

Total Value

Page Totals:	How Many	Total Value

COLLECTOR'S VALUE GUIDE™

87

Booster Card Series 3

Dark Network™ (Bo-158)

Value $_____
How Many
Total Value

Devidramon™ (Bo-132)

Value $_____
How Many
Total Value

Devil Chip™ (Bo-151)

Value $_____
How Many
Total Value

Disregard This!™ (Bo-161)

Value $_____
How Many
Total Value

Fake Betamon™ (Bo-124)

Value $_____
How Many
Total Value

Fake Drimogemon™ (Bo-130)

Value $_____
How Many
Total Value

Page Totals: How Many — Total Value

COLLECTOR'S VALUE GUIDE™

88

Booster Card Series 3

Floppy Disk™ (Bo-150)

Value
$_____

How Many

Total Value

Flymon™ (Bo-128)

Value
$_____

How Many

Total Value

Garurumon™ (Bo-120)

Value
$_____

How Many

Total Value

Gelemon™ (Bo-138)

Value
$_____

How Many

Total Value

Guardmon™ (Bo-113)

Value
$_____

How Many

Total Value

Hand From The Dark!™ (Bo-159)

Value
$_____

How Many

Total Value

Page Totals:	How Many	Total Value

COLLECTOR'S VALUE GUIDE™

Booster Card Series 3

Icemon™ (Bo-129)

Value $_____

How Many

Total Value

Igamon™ (Bo-123)

Value $_____

How Many

Total Value

Jijimon™ (Bo-145)

Value $_____

How Many

Total Value

Knightmon™ (Bo-114)

Value $_____

How Many

Total Value

Lillymon™ (Bo-140)

Value $_____

How Many

Total Value

Machinedramon™ (Bo-136)

Value $_____

How Many

Total Value

Foil

Page Totals:	How Many	Total Value

COLLECTOR'S VALUE GUIDE™

Booster Card Series 3

MagnaAngemon™ (Bo-142)

Value $_____
How Many _____
Total Value _____
Foil

MetalGarurumon™ (Bo-109)

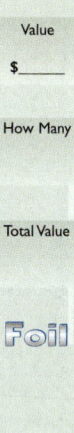

Value $_____
How Many _____
Total Value _____
Foil

MetalGreymon™ (Bo-115)

Value $_____
How Many _____
Total Value _____
Foil

MetalTyrannomon™ (Bo-133)

Value $_____
How Many _____
Total Value _____
Foil

Meteoritemon™ (Bo-141)

Value $_____
How Many _____
Total Value _____

MoliShellmon™ (Bo-121)

Value $_____
How Many _____
Total Value _____

COLLECTOR'S VALUE GUIDE™

Page Totals: How Many _____ Total Value _____

91

Booster Card Series 3

Penmon™ (Bo-116)

Value $_____
How Many
Total Value

PlatinaSukamon™ (Bo-118)

Value $_____
How Many
Total Value

PoisonKunemon™ (Bo-117)

Value $_____
How Many
Total Value

RedKokatorimon™ (Bo-134)

Value $_____
How Many
Total Value

Resurrection From The Dark!!™ (Bo-162)

Value $_____
How Many
Total Value

Saberdolamon™ (Bo-125)

Value $_____
How Many
Total Value

Page Totals: How Many ___ Total Value ___

COLLECTOR'S VALUE GUIDE™

Booster Card Series 3

Saikemon™ (Bo-119)

Value $____

How Many

Total Value

Seed Of Health™ (Bo-153)

Value $____

How Many

Total Value

Seed Of Speed™ (Bo-154)

Value $____

How Many

Total Value

Seed Of Strength™ (Bo-152)

Value $____

How Many

Total Value

SnowAgumon™ (Bo-126)

Value $____

How Many

Total Value

ToyAgumon™ (Bo-110)

Value $____

How Many

Total Value

COLLECTOR'S VALUE GUIDE™

Page Totals: | How Many | Total Value

93

Booster Card Series 3

Tsuchidalumon™ (Bo-137)

Value $ _____

How Many _____

Total Value _____

Tsukaimon™ (Bo-122)

Value $ _____

How Many _____

Total Value _____

Vademon™ (Bo-144)

Value $ _____

How Many _____

Total Value _____

Vamilimon™ (Bo-139)

Value $ _____

How Many _____

Total Value _____

Vegiemon™ (Bo-135)

Value $ _____

How Many _____

Total Value _____

We Are Honor Students™ (Bo-160)

Value $ _____

How Many _____

Total Value _____

Page Totals:	How Many	Total Value

COLLECTOR'S VALUE GUIDE™

94

Booster Card Series 3

Winning Percentage 40%!™ (Bo-155)

Value $_____
How Many
Total Value

Winning Percentage 60%!™ (Bo-156)

Value $_____
How Many
Total Value

Page Totals:	How Many	Total Value

American Trading Cards
Series One

This exciting 43-card series features characters from the Fox Kids program "Digimon: Digital Monsters." The set consists of 34 cards with parallel holofoil counterparts and 8 Ultimate Digimon cards for collectors to chase down. This set was released in Exclusive Preview and Unlimited editions. The Exclusive Preview edition featured an added bonus – a parallel set of gold-colored cards that are numbered 1–100. With only 3,400 of these cards out there, they are hard to find!

Agumon™ (11 of 34)

	Value	How Many	Total Value
★	$1.50		
☆	$4.00		
☆	$0.60		
★	$1.25		
★	$225.00		

Angemon™ (33 of 34)

	Value	How Many	Total Value
★	$1.50		
☆	$4.00		
☆	$0.70		
★	$3.00		
★	$130.00		

Bakemon™ (32 of 34)

	Value	How Many	Total Value
★	$1.50		
☆	$4.00		
☆	$0.70		
★	$3.25		
★	$130.00		

Birdramon™ (23 of 34)

	Value	How Many	Total Value
★	$1.50		
☆	$4.00		
☆	$0.40		
★	$1.25		
★	$130.00		

★ Ex. Preview Reg.   ☆ Ex. Preview Holofoil   ☆ Unlimited Ed. Reg.   ★ Unlimited Ed. Holofoil   ★ Gold

Page Totals:

COLLECTOR'S VALUE GUIDE™

American Trading Cards

Biyomon™ (13 of 34)

	Value	How Many	Total Value
★	$1.50		
☆	$4.00		
★	$0.45		
☆	$2.00		
★	$130.00		

Cockatrimon™ (34 of 34)

	Value	How Many	Total Value
★	$1.50		
☆	$4.00		
★	$0.65		
☆	$2.50		
★	$165.00		

Devimon™ (30 of 34)

	Value	How Many	Total Value
★	$1.50		
☆	$4.00		
★	$0.85		
☆	$2.25		
★	$200.00		

Digimon Checklist™ (N/A)

	Value	How Many	Total Value
★	$1.50		
☆	N/E		

Digivolve! Champions!!™ (3 of 34)

	Value	How Many	Total Value
★	$1.50		
☆	$4.00		
★	$0.45		
☆	$1.25		
★	$110.00		

Frigimon™ (31 of 34)

	Value	How Many	Total Value
★	$1.50		
☆	$4.00		
★	$0.60		
☆	$2.00		
★	$130.00		

★ Ex. Preview Reg. ☆ Ex. Preview Holofoil ★ Unlimited Ed. Reg. ☆ Unlimited Ed. Holofoil ★ Gold

COLLECTOR'S VALUE GUIDE™

Page Totals:	How Many	Total Value

American Trading Cards

Gabumon™ (12 of 34)

	Value	How Many	Total Value
★	$1.50		
☆	$4.00		
☆	$0.60		
★	$2.00		
★	$165.00		

Garurumon™ (20 of 34)

	Value	How Many	Total Value
★	$1.50		
☆	$4.00		
☆	$0.50		
★	$2.25		
★	$250.00		

Gomamon™ (16 of 34)

	Value	How Many	Total Value
★	$1.50		
☆	$4.00		
☆	$0.75		
★	$1.50		
★	$130.00		

Greymon™ (19 of 34)

	Value	How Many	Total Value
★	$1.50		
☆	$4.00		
☆	$0.60		
★	$2.75		
★	$225.00		

Ikkakumon™ (27 of 34)

	Value	How Many	Total Value
★	$1.50		
☆	$4.00		
☆	$0.50		
★	$1.75		
★	$130.00		

Izzy & Motimon™ (7 of 34)

	Value	How Many	Total Value
★	$1.50		
☆	$4.00		
☆	$0.50		
★	$1.75		
★	$200.00		

★ Ex. Preview Reg. ☆ Ex. Preview Holofoil ☆ Unlimited Ed. Reg. ★ Unlimited Ed. Holofoil ★ Gold

Page Totals: | How Many | Total Value |

COLLECTOR'S VALUE GUIDE™

American Trading Cards

Joe & Bukamon™ (9 of 34)

	Value	How Many	Total Value
★	$1.50		
☆	$4.00		
☆	$0.50		
★	$1.75		
★	$100.00		

Kabuterimon™ (25 of 34)

	Value	How Many	Total Value
★	$1.50		
☆	$4.00		
☆	$0.65		
★	$2.25		
★	$130.00		

Kuwagamon™ (18 of 34)

	Value	How Many	Total Value
★	$1.50		
☆	$4.00		
☆	$0.45		
★	$1.50		
★	$130.00		

Leomon™ (28 of 34)

	Value	How Many	Total Value
★	$1.50		
☆	$4.00		
☆	$0.75		
★	$2.75		
★	$150.00		

Matt & Tsunomon™ (5 of 34)

	Value	How Many	Total Value
★	$1.50		
☆	$4.00		
☆	$0.50		
★	$1.75		
★	$100.00		

Meramon™ (24 of 34)

	Value	How Many	Total Value
★	$1.50		
☆	$4.00		
☆	$0.45		
★	$1.25		
★	$130.00		

★ Ex. Preview Reg. ☆ Ex. Preview Holofoil ☆ Unlimited Ed. Reg. ★ Unlimited Ed. Holofoil ★ Gold

COLLECTOR'S VALUE GUIDE™

Page Totals: | How Many | Total Value

American Trading Cards

Mimi & Tanemon™ (8 of 34)

	Value	How Many	Total Value
★	$1.50		
☆	$4.00		
☆	$0.55		
☆	$1.75		
★	$100.00		

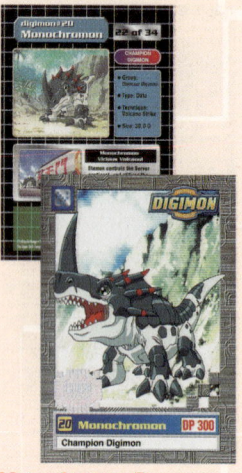

Monochromon™ (22 of 34)

	Value	How Many	Total Value
★	$1.50		
☆	$4.00		
☆	$0.40		
☆	$1.00		
★	$170.00		

Ogremon™ (29 of 34)

	Value	How Many	Total Value
★	$1.50		
☆	$4.00		
☆	$0.50		
☆	$1.50		
★	$140.00		

Palmon™ (15 of 34)

	Value	How Many	Total Value
★	$1.50		
☆	$4.00		
☆	$0.60		
☆	$1.50		
★	$150.00		

Patamon™ (17 of 34)

	Value	How Many	Total Value
★	$1.50		
☆	$4.00		
☆	$0.60		
☆	$1.50		
★	$130.00		

Ready for battle! Rookies!!™ (2 of 34)

	Value	How Many	Total Value
★	$1.50		
☆	$4.00		
☆	$0.40		
☆	$1.25		
★	$130.00		

★ Ex. Preview Reg.   ☆ Ex. Preview Holofoil   ☆ Unlimited Ed. Reg.   ☆ Unlimited Ed. Holofoil   ★ Gold

Page Totals:

How Many	Total Value

American Trading Cards

Seadramon™ (21 of 34)

	Value	How Many	Total Value
★	$1.50		
☆	$4.00		
☆	$0.50		
★	$1.75		
★	$185.00		

Selected Kids!™ (1 of 34)

	Value	How Many	Total Value
★	$1.50		
☆	$4.00		
☆	$0.50		
★	$1.50		
★	$130.00		

Sora & Yokomon™ (6 of 34)

	Value	How Many	Total Value
★	$1.50		
☆	$4.00		
☆	$0.50		
★	$1.50		
★	$100.00		

T.K. & Tokomon™ (10 of 34)

	Value	How Many	Total Value
★	$1.50		
☆	$4.00		
☆	$0.40		
★	$1.00		
★	$100.00		

Tai & Koromon™ (4 of 34)

	Value	How Many	Total Value
★	$1.50		
☆	$4.00		
☆	$0.40		
★	$2.25		
★	$150.00		

Tentomon™ (14 of 34)

	Value	How Many	Total Value
★	$1.50		
☆	$4.00		
☆	$0.50		
★	$1.50		
★	$130.00		

★ Ex. Preview Reg.   ☆ Ex. Preview Holofoil   ☆ Unlimited Ed. Reg.   ★ Unlimited Ed. Holofoil   ★ Gold

COLLECTOR'S VALUE GUIDE™

Page Totals:	How Many	Total Value

American Trading Cards

Togemon™ (26 of 34)

	Value	How Many	Total Value
★	$1.50		
★	$4.00		
★	$0.50		
★	$2.75		
★	$130.00		

Andromon™ (U1 of 8)

	Value	How Many	Total Value
★	$17.00		
★	$10.00		

Etemon™ (U3 of 8)

	Value	How Many	Total Value
★	$17.00		
★	$10.00		

MegaKabuterimon™ (U8 of 8)

	Value	How Many	Total Value
★	$17.00		
★	$10.00		

MetalGreymon™ (U6 of 8)

	Value	How Many	Total Value
★	$17.00		
★	$10.00		

Monzaemon™ (U2 of 8)

	Value	How Many	Total Value
★	$17.00		
★	$10.00		

★ Ex. Preview Reg. ★ Ex. Preview Holofoil ★ Unlimited Ed. Reg. ★ Unlimited Ed. Holofoil ★ Gold

Page Totals:

COLLECTOR'S
Value Guide™

American Trading Cards

Piximon™ (U5 of 8)

	Value	How Many	Total Value
☆	$17.00		
☆	$10.00		

SkullGreymon™ (U4 of 8)

	Value	How Many	Total Value
☆	$17.00		
☆	$10.00		

WereGarurumon™ (U7 of 8)

	Value	How Many	Total Value
☆	$17.00		
☆	$10.00		

American Trading Cards Series 2

May 2000 saw the release of a second set of American Trading Cards. Series 2 consists of 32 regular cards as well as 10 special card inserts numbered D1–D10. As an added bonus, there are special Japanese-text holofoil insert cards to collect; a holofoil parallel series and, as in Series 1, extremely rare gold-card versions of each of the 32 regular cards. Each gold card is numbered 1–100. Since these cards are new in the marketplace, secondary market values have not yet been established for them.

Assault! Messenger From The Dark!™ (32 of 32)

	Value	How Many	Total Value
☆	N/E		
☆	N/E		
☆	N/E		

★ Ex. Preview Reg. ★ Ex. Preview Holofoil ★ Unlimited Ed. Reg. ★ Unlimited Ed. Holofoil ★ Gold

COLLECTOR'S VALUE GUIDE™

Page Totals:	How Many	Total Value

American Trading Cards

Bonds Of Friendship!™
(1 of 32)

	Value	How Many	Total Value
☆	N/E		
★	N/E		
★	N/E		

Crash! Street Battle!™
(30 of 32)

	Value	How Many	Total Value
☆	N/E		
★	N/E		
★	N/E		

Datamon™ (15 of 32)

	Value	How Many	Total Value
☆	N/E		
★	N/E		
★	N/E		

DemiDevimon™ (4 of 32)

	Value	How Many	Total Value
☆	N/E		
★	N/E		
★	N/E		

Devidramon™ (11 of 32)

	Value	How Many	Total Value
☆	N/E		
★	N/E		
★	N/E		

Digimon Checklist™ (N/A)

	Value	How Many	Total Value
☆	N/E		

★ Ex. Preview Reg.   ★ Ex. Preview Holofoil   ★ Unlimited Ed. Reg.   ★ Unlimited Ed. Holofoil   ★ Gold

Page Totals:	How Many	Total Value

COLLECTOR'S VALUE GUIDE™

American Trading Cards

Digivolve To Ultimate!™
(25 of 32)

	Value	How Many	Total Value
☆	N/E		
★	N/E		
★	N/E		

Dokugumon™ (12 of 32)

	Value	How Many	Total Value
☆	N/E		
★	N/E		
★	N/E		

Fly! The Loving Sky!™
(28 of 32)

	Value	How Many	Total Value
☆	N/E		
★	N/E		
★	N/E		

Flymon™ (8 of 32)

	Value	How Many	Total Value
☆	N/E		
★	N/E		
★	N/E		

Garudamon™ (18 of 32)

	Value	How Many	Total Value
☆	N/E		
★	N/E		
★	N/E		

Gatomon™ (9 of 32)

	Value	How Many	Total Value
☆	N/E		
★	N/E		
★	N/E		

★ Ex. Preview Reg.   ☆ Ex. Preview Holofoil   ★ Unlimited Ed. Reg.   ★ Unlimited Ed. Holofoil   ★ Gold

COLLECTOR'S VALUE GUIDE™

Page Totals:	How Many	Total Value

105

American Trading Cards

Gekomon™ (7 of 32)

	Value	How Many	Total Value
☆	N/E		
☆	N/E		
☆	N/E		

Gennai™ (2 of 32)

	Value	How Many	Total Value
☆	N/E		
☆	N/E		
☆	N/E		

Gesomon™ (13 of 32)

	Value	How Many	Total Value
☆	N/E		
☆	N/E		
☆	N/E		

Hot Battle! Strong Courage!™ (29 of 32)

	Value	How Many	Total Value
☆	N/E		
☆	N/E		
☆	N/E		

Kari Kamiya™ (3 of 32)

	Value	How Many	Total Value
☆	N/E		
☆	N/E		
☆	N/E		

Lillymon™ (21 of 32)

	Value	How Many	Total Value
☆	N/E		
☆	N/E		
☆	N/E		

★ Ex. Preview Reg. ☆ Ex. Preview Holofoil ☆ Unlimited Ed. Reg. ★ Unlimited Ed. Holofoil ★ Gold

Page Totals: | How Many | Total Value

COLLECTOR'S Value Guide™

American Trading Cards

Mammothmon™ (19 of 32)

	Value	How Many	Total Value
☆	N/E		
☆	N/E		
☆	N/E		

MegaSeadramon™ (24 of 32)

	Value	How Many	Total Value
☆	N/E		
☆	N/E		
☆	N/E		

Myotismon™ (16 of 32)

	Value	How Many	Total Value
☆	N/E		
☆	N/E		
☆	N/E		

Nanimon™ (10 of 32)

	Value	How Many	Total Value
☆	N/E		
☆	N/E		
☆	N/E		

Penetrate! Evil Dimension!™ (27 of 32)

	Value	How Many	Total Value
☆	N/E		
☆	N/E		
☆	N/E		

Phantomon™ (22 of 32)

	Value	How Many	Total Value
☆	N/E		
☆	N/E		
☆	N/E		

★ Ex. Preview Reg.   ☆ Ex. Preview Holofoil   ★ Unlimited Ed. Reg.   ☆ Unlimited Ed. Holofoil   ★ Gold

COLLECTOR'S VALUE GUIDE™

Page Totals:	How Many	Total Value

American Trading Cards

Rip Up! Perfect Claw!™
(26 of 32)

	Value	How Many	Total Value
☆	N/E		
☆	N/E		
★	N/E		

SkullMeramon™
(20 of 32)

	Value	How Many	Total Value
☆	N/E		
☆	N/E		
★	N/E		

Tyrannomon™ (5 of 32)

	Value	How Many	Total Value
☆	N/E		
☆	N/E		
★	N/E		

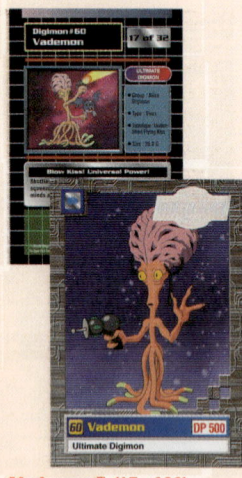

Vademon™ (17 of 32)

	Value	How Many	Total Value
☆	N/E		
☆	N/E		
★	N/E		

Vegiemon™ (6 of 32)

	Value	How Many	Total Value
☆	N/E		
☆	N/E		
★	N/E		

Violent Shock! Decisive Battle!™ (31 of 32)

	Value	How Many	Total Value
☆	N/E		
☆	N/E		
★	N/E		

★ Ex. Preview Reg.   ☆ Ex. Preview Holofoil   ☆ Unlimited Ed. Reg.   ☆ Unlimited Ed. Holofoil   ★ Gold

Page Totals:	How Many	Total Value

COLLECTOR'S VALUE GUIDE™

American Trading Cards

Wizardmon™ (14 of 32)

	Value	How Many	Total Value
☆	N/E		
✦	N/E		
★	N/E		

Zudomon™ (23 of 32)

	Value	How Many	Total Value
☆	N/E		
✦	N/E		
★	N/E		

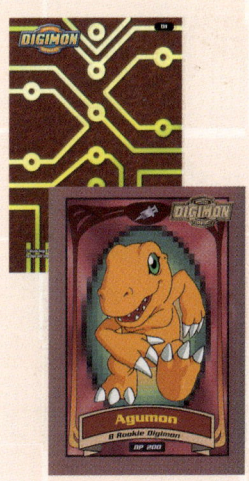

Agumon™ (D1)

	Value	How Many	Total Value
✦	N/E		

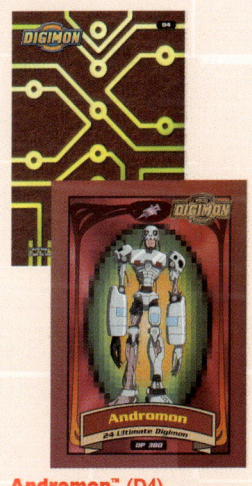

Andromon™ (D4)

	Value	How Many	Total Value
✦	N/E		

Digitamamon™ (D9)

	Value	How Many	Total Value
✦	N/E		

Drimogemon™ (D7)

	Value	How Many	Total Value
✦	N/E		

PHOTO UNAVAILABLE

★ Ex. Preview Reg. ☆ Ex. Preview Holofoil ✦ Unlimited Ed. Reg. ✧ Unlimited Ed. Holofoil ★ Gold

COLLECTOR'S VALUE GUIDE™

Page Totals:	How Many	Total Value

109

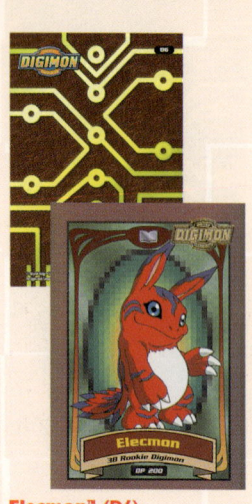

American Trading Cards

Elecmon™ (D6)

	Value	How Many	Total Value
★	N/E		

Gazimon™ (D8)

	Value	How Many	Total Value
★	N/E		

Gomamon™ (D2)

	Value	How Many	Total Value
★	N/E		

Kuwagamon™ (D3)

	Value	How Many	Total Value
★	N/E		

ShogunGekomon™ (D10)

	Value	How Many	Total Value
★	N/E		

Unimon™ (D5)

	Value	How Many	Total Value
★	N/E		

PHOTO UNAVAILABLE

★ Ex. Preview Reg. ★ Ex. Preview Holofoil ★ Unlimited Ed. Reg. ★ Unlimited Ed. Holofoil ★ Gold

Page Totals:	How Many	Total Value

COLLECTOR'S VALUE GUIDE™

Japanese Trading Cards
Trading Collection Light Series 1

These Japanese Digimon trading cards are based on the Japanese "Digimon Adventure" television show. They feature scenes from various episodes, much like the American trading cards. There are 54 cards in the set, including nine holofoil cards. The non-foil cards are numbered from 1–45, while the holofoil cards are identified as P1–P9. These colorful cards can be bought in 10-card blue-colored packs that include nine regular cards and one holofoil.

Am I A Leader?!™ (36)

Value $_____ | How Many | Total Value

Beat Him Up, Greymon!!™ (08)

Value $_____ | How Many | Total Value

Brother!™ (11)

Value $_____ | How Many | Total Value

Cheer Up, Joe!™ (25)

Value $_____ | How Many | Total Value

Deadly Foxfire!™ (13)

Value $_____ | How Many | Total Value

Devimon's Desire™ (27)

Value $_____ | How Many | Total Value

Page Totals: | How Many | Total Value

Japanese Trading Cards

111

Japanese Trading Cards

Discovery Of Invader™ (19)

Value $_____ How Many Total Value

Don't Eat!!™ (38)

Value $_____ How Many Total Value

Don't Ignore Us!!™ (35)

Value $_____ How Many Total Value

Dream Is Gone . . .™ (28)

Value $_____ How Many Total Value

Evolved Palmon! Togemon!!™ (23)

Value $_____ How Many Total Value

Final Battle!™ (43)

Value $_____ How Many Total Value

Get Power Together!™ (44)

Value $_____ How Many Total Value

Glowing Digivice!!™ (29)

Value $_____ How Many Total Value

Go! Kabuterimon!!™ (21)

Value $_____ How Many Total Value

Page Totals: How Many Total Value

COLLECTOR'S VALUE GUIDE™

Japanese Trading Cards

Going To A New Continent!™ (45)
Value How Many Total Value
$_____

Have A Mega Flame!!™ (09)
Value How Many Total Value
$_____

He's Coming!!™ (07)
Value How Many Total Value
$_____

I Can't Evolve . . .™ (41)
Value How Many Total Value
$_____

I Will Help Yamato!™ (12)
Value How Many Total Value
$_____

I Will Save You This Time!!™ (16)
Value How Many Total Value
$_____

Leave It To Me!™ (33)
Value How Many Total Value
$_____

Let's Join Forces!™ (03)
Value How Many Total Value
$_____

Spiral Sword™ (20)
Value How Many Total Value
$_____

Page Totals: How Many Total Value

COLLECTOR'S VALUE GUIDE™

Japanese Trading Cards

Taichi, Dangerous!!™ (02)

Value	How Many	Total Value
$		

Takeru, Where Are You!!™ (32)

Value	How Many	Total Value
$		

There Is A Deserted Factory!™ (18)

Value	How Many	Total Value
$		

This Sounds Nice . . .™ (10)

Value	How Many	Total Value
$		

Togemon Vs. Monzaemon™ (24)

Value	How Many	Total Value
$		

Wait, Both Of You!™ (26)

Value	How Many	Total Value
$		

We Are Saved . . .™ (39)

Value	How Many	Total Value
$		

Welcome To Tokomon Village™ (14)

Value	How Many	Total Value
$		

Wh . . . Who Are You?™ (34)

Value	How Many	Total Value
$		

Page Totals:

How Many	Total Value

COLLECTOR'S VALUE GUIDE™

Japanese Trading Cards

What? A Public Telephone?!™ (06)

Value	How Many	Total Value
$		

What Are You?!™ (01)

Value	How Many	Total Value
$		

Where Is Everybody?™ (40)

Value	How Many	Total Value
$		

Why Did You Evolve?™ (05)

Value	How Many	Total Value
$		

Why Is A Teddy Bear Attacking Us!™ (22)

Value	How Many	Total Value
$		

Wow!™ (42)

Value	How Many	Total Value
$		

Wow! They're Coming!!™ (37)

Value	How Many	Total Value
$		

Yes! Agumon!!™ (04)

Value	How Many	Total Value
$		

Yes! Birdramon!!™ (17)

Value	How Many	Total Value
$		

	How Many	Total Value
Page Totals:		

COLLECTOR'S VALUE GUIDE™

115

Japanese Trading Cards

You Are An Important Partner!™ (15)

Value	How Many	Total Value
$		

You Don't Know Anything About Me!™ (30)

Value	How Many	Total Value
$		

You, Too!!™ (31)

Value	How Many	Total Value
$		

Devimon™ (P9)

Value	How Many	Total Value
$6.00		

Joe's Partner™ (P7)

Value	How Many	Total Value
$6.00		

Koshiro's Partner™ (P4)

Value	How Many	Total Value
$6.00		

Leomon And Ogremon™ (P8)

Value	How Many	Total Value
$6.00		

Mimi's Partner™ (P5)

Value	How Many	Total Value
$6.00		

Sora's Partner™ (P2)

Value	How Many	Total Value
$6.00		

Page Totals:

How Many	Total Value

COLLECTOR'S VALUE GUIDE™

Taichi's Partner™ (P1)

Value	How Many	Total Value
$6.00		

Takeru's Partner™ (P6)

Value	How Many	Total Value
$6.00		

Yamato's Partner™ (P3)

Value	How Many	Total Value
$6.00		

Japanese Trading Cards

COLLECTOR'S
VALUE GUIDE™

Page Totals:	How Many	Total Value

Japanese Trading Cards
Trading Collection Light
Series 2

Like the first series of Japanese trading cards, the Trading Collection Light Series 2 cards are based on the Japanese "Digimon Adventure" television show. There are 121 cards in this series, including nine holofoil cards and 72 puzzle cards. The remaining 40 cards are numbered from 46 to 85 and feature recognizable scenes and familiar characters from the television show.

Be Ready! Chosen Children!!™ (51)

Value	How Many	Total Value
$		

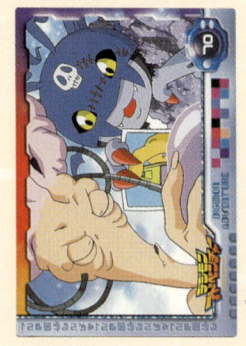

Can I Have A Crest, Please?™ (70)

Value	How Many	Total Value
$		

Come On Everybody! Follow Me!!™ (53)

Value	How Many	Total Value
$		

Do You Think You Can Defeat Me?™ (57)

Value	How Many	Total Value
$		

Don't Worry About Me. Just Go . . .™ (66)

Value	How Many	Total Value
$		

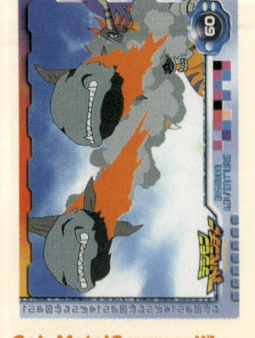

Go! MetalGreymon!!™ (60)

Value	How Many	Total Value
$		

Page Totals: | How Many | Total Value

COLLECTOR'S VALUE GUIDE™

Japanese Trading Cards

Hurry Up! The Gate Is Closing!!™ (78)

Value	How Many	Total Value
$		

I Can't Lose™ (58)

Value	How Many	Total Value
$		

I Don't Want To Go!!™ (72)

Value	How Many	Total Value
$		

I Have Been Waiting For You, Chosen Children™ (56)

Value	How Many	Total Value
$		

I Have To Go . . .™ (62)

Value	How Many	Total Value
$		

I Protect Koshiro!™ (71)

Value	How Many	Total Value
$		

I'll Never Fail To Get A Crest!!™ (69)

Value	How Many	Total Value
$		

I'll Save You Now, Joe!!™ (67)

Value	How Many	Total Value
$		

I'm The Strongest Digimon™ (47)

Value	How Many	Total Value
$		

COLLECTOR'S VALUE GUIDE™

Page Totals: | How Many | Total Value |

Japanese Trading Cards

I Will Kill You!™ (75)

Value $_____ | How Many | Total Value

I Will Take The Crests From The Children™ (64)

Value $_____ | How Many | Total Value

Let's Find The Rest Of Our Friends!™ (68)

Value $_____ | How Many | Total Value

Let's Go Find The Last One!!™ (80)

Value $_____ | How Many | Total Value

Let's Sneak In!™ (77)

Value $_____ | How Many | Total Value

My Crest Doesn't Glow!™ (74)

Value $_____ | How Many | Total Value

My Tag Is Glowing!™ (48)

Value $_____ | How Many | Total Value

Oh My God! They Found Us!!™ (85)

Value $_____ | How Many | Total Value

Oh, No! A Monster!!™ (82)

Value $_____ | How Many | Total Value

Page Totals: | How Many | Total Value

COLLECTOR'S VALUE GUIDE™

120

Japanese Trading Cards

Pretend You're Stuffed Animals™ (84)

Value | How Many | Total Value
$_____

Save Mimi!!™ (73)

Value | How Many | Total Value
$_____

Stop! Greymon!!™ (50)

Value | How Many | Total Value
$_____

Super Evolution! Garudamon!!™ (76)

Value | How Many | Total Value
$_____

Take That!™ (52)

Value | How Many | Total Value
$_____

The Sender Should Be Here!™ (55)

Value | How Many | Total Value
$_____

This Is It! Is This Further Evolution!!™ (59)

Value | How Many | Total Value
$_____

This Is My Crest!™ (54)

Value | How Many | Total Value
$_____

This Scene . . . I've Seen It Before™ (83)

Value | How Many | Total Value
$_____

Page Totals:	How Many	Total Value

COLLECTOR'S VALUE GUIDE™

Japanese Trading Cards

Welcome To Pagumon Village!™ (46)
Value $_____ How Many _____ Total Value _____

What Should We Do . . . ?™ (79)
Value $_____ How Many _____ Total Value _____

Where Is The Eighth Child?™ (81)
Value $_____ How Many _____ Total Value _____

Work Harder!!™ (65)
Value $_____ How Many _____ Total Value _____

Yes! I'm Back!!™ (61)
Value $_____ How Many _____ Total Value _____

You Are Alive, Taichi!!™ (63)
Value $_____ How Many _____ Total Value _____

Puzzle Cards

One colorful and exciting holofoil card is included in every package of Trading Collection Light Series 2 cards. These cards are numbered from P1–P9. They depict each of the Digi-destined and their Digimon, as well as a group of some of the "bad" Digimon.

In addition to the regular trading and holofoil cards, Trading Collection Light Series 2 contains 72 puzzle cards, which can be seen beginning on page 124. Each is part of a group of nine that, when placed together, forms a picture identical to one of the holofoil cards of the Digi-destined seen on page 123.

Page Totals: How Many _____ Total Value _____

COLLECTOR'S VALUE GUIDE™

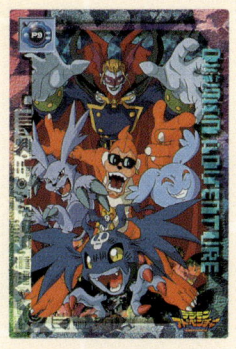

Japanese Trading Cards

Bad Digimon™ (P9)
Value: $7.00 | How Many | Total Value

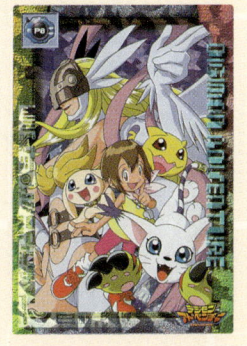

Hikari™ (P8)
Value: $7.00 | How Many | Total Value

Joe™ (P7)
Value: $7.00 | How Many | Total Value

Koshiro™ (P4)
Value: $7.00 | How Many | Total Value

Mimi™ (P6)
Value: $7.00 | How Many | Total Value

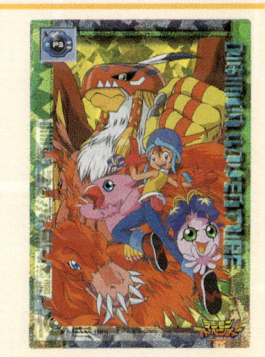

Sora™ (P3)
Value: $7.00 | How Many | Total Value

Taichi™ (P1)
Value: $7.00 | How Many | Total Value

Takeru™ (P5)
Value: $7.00 | How Many | Total Value

Yamato™ (P2)
Value: $7.00 | How Many | Total Value

Page Totals: How Many | Total Value

COLLECTOR'S VALUE GUIDE™

123

Japanese Trading Cards

Hikari™ (Puzzle Card 64)
Value $____ How Many Total Value

Hikari™ (Puzzle Card 65)
Value $____ How Many Total Value

Hikari™ (Puzzle Card 66)
Value $____ How Many Total Value

Hikari™ (Puzzle Card 67)
Value $____ How Many Total Value

Hikari™ (Puzzle Card 68)
Value $____ How Many Total Value

Hikari™ (Puzzle Card 69)
Value $____ How Many Total Value

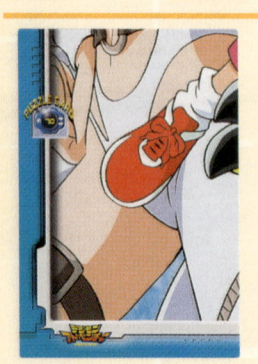

Hikari™ (Puzzle Card 70)
Value $____ How Many Total Value

Hikari™ (Puzzle Card 71)
Value $____ How Many Total Value

Hikari™ (Puzzle Card 72)
Value $____ How Many Total Value

Page Totals: How Many | Total Value

COLLECTOR'S VALUE GUIDE™

Japanese Trading Cards

Joe™ (Puzzle Card 55)

Value	How Many	Total Value
$____		

Joe™ (Puzzle Card 56)

Value	How Many	Total Value
$____		

Joe™ (Puzzle Card 57)

Value	How Many	Total Value
$____		

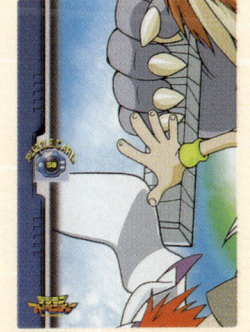

Joe™ (Puzzle Card 58)

Value	How Many	Total Value
$____		

Joe™ (Puzzle Card 59)

Value	How Many	Total Value
$____		

Joe™ (Puzzle Card 60)

Value	How Many	Total Value
$____		

Joe™ (Puzzle Card 61)

Value	How Many	Total Value
$____		

Joe™ (Puzzle Card 62)

Value	How Many	Total Value
$____		

Joe™ (Puzzle Card 63)

Value	How Many	Total Value
$____		

COLLECTOR'S VALUE GUIDE™

Page Totals:	How Many	Total Value

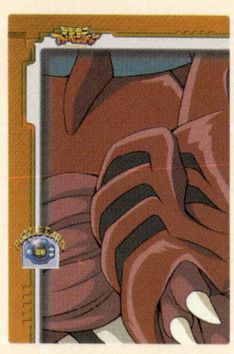

Japanese Trading Cards

Koshiro™ (Puzzle Card 28)

Value $_____ | How Many | Total Value

Koshiro™ (Puzzle Card 29)

Value $_____ | How Many | Total Value

Koshiro™ (Puzzle Card 30)

Value $_____ | How Many | Total Value

Koshiro™ (Puzzle Card 31)

Value $_____ | How Many | Total Value

Koshiro™ (Puzzle Card 32)

Value $_____ | How Many | Total Value

Koshiro™ (Puzzle Card 33)

Value $_____ | How Many | Total Value

Koshiro™ (Puzzle Card 34)

Value $_____ | How Many | Total Value

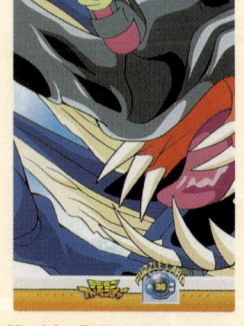

Koshiro™ (Puzzle Card 35)

Value $_____ | How Many | Total Value

Koshiro™ (Puzzle Card 36)

Value $_____ | How Many | Total Value

Page Totals: | How Many | Total Value

COLLECTOR'S VALUE GUIDE™

Mimi™ (Puzzle Card 46)

| Value $____ | How Many | Total Value |

Mimi™ (Puzzle Card 47)

| Value $____ | How Many | Total Value |

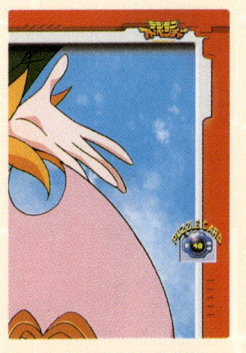

Mimi™ (Puzzle Card 48)

| Value $____ | How Many | Total Value |

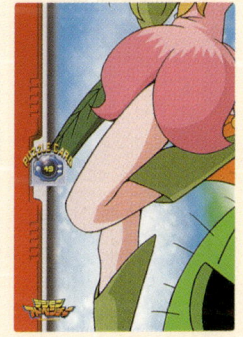

Mimi™ (Puzzle Card 49)

| Value $____ | How Many | Total Value |

Mimi™ (Puzzle Card 50)

| Value $____ | How Many | Total Value |

Mimi™ (Puzzle Card 51)

| Value $____ | How Many | Total Value |

Mimi™ (Puzzle Card 52)

| Value $____ | How Many | Total Value |

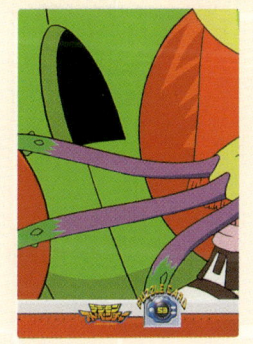

Mimi™ (Puzzle Card 53)

| Value $____ | How Many | Total Value |

Mimi™ (Puzzle Card 54)

| Value $____ | How Many | Total Value |

Japanese Trading Cards

Page Totals: | How Many | Total Value |

COLLECTOR'S VALUE GUIDE™

127

Japanese Trading Cards

Sora™ (Puzzle Card 19)

Value	How Many	Total Value
$____		

Sora™ (Puzzle Card 20)

Value	How Many	Total Value
$____		

Sora™ (Puzzle Card 21)

Value	How Many	Total Value
$____		

Sora™ (Puzzle Card 22)

Value	How Many	Total Value
$____		

Sora™ (Puzzle Card 23)

Value	How Many	Total Value
$____		

Sora™ (Puzzle Card 24)

Value	How Many	Total Value
$____		

Sora™ (Puzzle Card 25)

Value	How Many	Total Value
$____		

Sora™ (Puzzle Card 26)

Value	How Many	Total Value
$____		

Sora™ (Puzzle Card 27)

Value	How Many	Total Value
$____		

Page Totals:

How Many	Total Value

COLLECTOR'S VALUE GUIDE™

Japanese Trading Cards

Taichi™ (Puzzle Card 01)

| Value $_____ | How Many | Total Value |

Taichi™ (Puzzle Card 02)

| Value $_____ | How Many | Total Value |

Taichi™ (Puzzle Card 03)

| Value $_____ | How Many | Total Value |

Taichi™ (Puzzle Card 04)

| Value $_____ | How Many | Total Value |

Taichi™ (Puzzle Card 05)

| Value $_____ | How Many | Total Value |

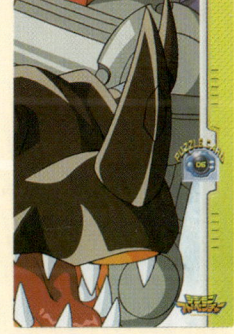

Taichi™ (Puzzle Card 06)

| Value $_____ | How Many | Total Value |

Taichi™ (Puzzle Card 07)

| Value $_____ | How Many | Total Value |

Taichi™ (Puzzle Card 08)

| Value $_____ | How Many | Total Value |

Taichi™ (Puzzle Card 09)

| Value $_____ | How Many | Total Value |

COLLECTOR'S VALUE GUIDE™

| Page Totals: | How Many | Total Value |

Japanese Trading Cards

Takeru™ (Puzzle Card 37)

| Value $____ | How Many | Total Value |

Takeru™ (Puzzle Card 38)

| Value $____ | How Many | Total Value |

Takeru™ (Puzzle Card 39)

| Value $____ | How Many | Total Value |

Takeru™ (Puzzle Card 40)

| Value $____ | How Many | Total Value |

Takeru™ (Puzzle Card 41)

| Value $____ | How Many | Total Value |

Takeru™ (Puzzle Card 42)

| Value $____ | How Many | Total Value |

Takeru™ (Puzzle Card 43)

| Value $____ | How Many | Total Value |

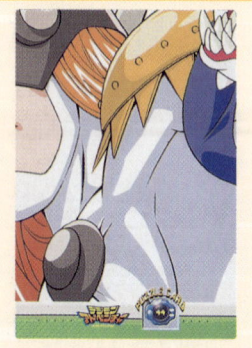

Takeru™ (Puzzle Card 44)

| Value $____ | How Many | Total Value |

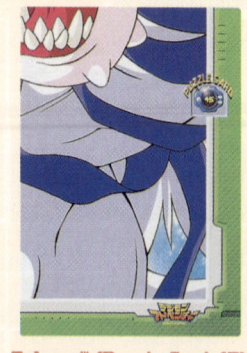

Takeru™ (Puzzle Card 45)

| Value $____ | How Many | Total Value |

Page Totals: | How Many | Total Value

COLLECTOR'S VALUE GUIDE™

Yamato™ (Puzzle Card 10)

Value	How Many	Total Value
$		

Yamato™ (Puzzle Card 11)

Value	How Many	Total Value
$		

Yamato™ (Puzzle Card 12)

Value	How Many	Total Value
$		

Yamato™ (Puzzle Card 13)

Value	How Many	Total Value
$		

Yamato™ (Puzzle Card 14)

Value	How Many	Total Value
$		

Yamato™ (Puzzle Card 15)

Value	How Many	Total Value
$		

Yamato™ (Puzzle Card 16)

Value	How Many	Total Value
$		

Yamato™ (Puzzle Card 17)

Value	How Many	Total Value
$		

Yamato™ (Puzzle Card 18)

Value	How Many	Total Value
$		

Japanese Trading Cards

COLLECTOR'S VALUE GUIDE™

Page Totals:	How Many	Total Value

Other American And Japanese Cards

There are several other series of Japanese and American cards available for the Digimon fan to collect and enjoy. Secondary market values have not yet been established for all of these cards, so where applicable, we have left a blank line for you to write in the values once they do become available.

Action Figure Promo Cards (American)

These five holofoil cards come packaged with 5-inch Digimon Digivolving Action Figures. Each Digimon is pictured on the front of the card in its evolution, while the back lists its statistics and features a smaller picture from the television show "Digimon: Digital Monsters."

	Market Value		Market Value
☐ Angemon™ (#43)	$12.00	☐ MetalGreymon™ (#54)	$12.00
☐ Garudamon™ (#65)	$12.00	☐ WereGarurumon™ (#56)	$16.00
☐ MegaKabuterimon™ (#87)	$12.00		

Fox Kids Introductory Series 1 (American)

Seven promotional cards were released by Fox Kids and Upper Deck along with the first "Digimon: Digital Monsters" video. The cards are similar to the Upper Deck trading cards and feature each Digi-destined child (except Kari) with his or her In-Training Digimon.

	Market Value		Market Value
☐ Izzy & Motimon™ (#4)	$_____	☐ Sora & Yokomon™ (#3)	$_____
☐ Joe & Bukamon™ (#6)	$_____	☐ T.K. & Tokomon™ (#7)	$_____
☐ Matt & Tsunomon™ (#2)	$_____	☐ Tai & Koromon™ (#1)	$_____
☐ Mimi & Tanemon™ (#5)	$_____		

Page Totals:	How Many	Total Value

CARD TACTICS (JAPANESE)

The Japanese Card Tactics battle card game is a unique combination of a card game and a computer game. There are 133 game cards in the set, which are purchased in booster packs, and the game is played with the help of a hand-held computer.

	Market Value		Market Value
☐ Adventure Tag™ (#261)	$_____	☐ Elecmon™ (#213)	$_____
☐ Agumon™ (#119)	$_____	☐ Emergency Provisions™ (#182)	$_____
☐ Andromon™ (#277)	$_____	☐ Emergency Provisions™ (#342)	$_____
☐ Angemon™ (#375)	$_____	☐ Emergency Provisions (Small)™ (#264)	$_____
☐ Angewomon™ (#295)	$_____	☐ Energy Loss™ (#358)	$_____
☐ Antivaccine Program™ (#369)	$_____	☐ Etemon™ (#270)	$_____
☐ AtolaKabuterimon™ (#362)	$_____	☐ Everybody's Here! Our Team Power Is Full Now!!™ (#194)	$_____
☐ Attack™ (#274)	$_____	☐ Fire Breath™ (#135)	$_____
☐ Back and Front Badge™ (#297)	$_____	☐ Flymon™ (#280)	$_____
☐ Birdramon™ (#291)	$_____	☐ Frigimon™ (#117)	$_____
☐ Biyomon™ (#214)	$_____	☐ Gabumon™ (#357)	$_____
☐ Black Gear™ (#202)	$_____	☐ Garudamon™ (#100)	$_____
☐ Centarumon™ (#122)	$_____	☐ Garurumon™ (#136)	$_____
☐ Cold Breath™ (#363)	$_____	☐ Gatomon™ (#286)	$_____
☐ CP Transmitting Pump™ (#114)	$_____	☐ Gazimon™ (#349)	$_____
☐ Data – DA™ (#126)	$_____	☐ Gennai™ (#109)	$_____
☐ Data Destruction Program™ (#294)	$_____	☐ Going Berserk™ (#260)	$_____
☐ Deathmeramon™ (#377)	$_____	☐ Gomamon™ (#139)	$_____
☐ DemiDevimon™ (#108)	$_____	☐ Greymon™ (#275)	$_____
☐ Deterioration™ (#273)	$_____	☐ Ikkakumon™ (#359)	$_____
☐ Devidramon™ (#112)	$_____	☐ Illegal Drink™ (#348)	$_____
☐ Devimon™ (#218)	$_____	☐ Instant Hospitalization™ (#367)	$_____
☐ Digital Injection™ (#347)	$_____	☐ Kabuterimon™ (#190)	$_____
☐ Digitamamon™ (#352)	$_____	☐ Kokatorimon™ (#192)	$_____
☐ Digivice™ (#216)	$_____	☐ Koshiro's Analysis™ (#110)	$_____
☐ Dokugumon™ (#272)	$_____	☐ Koshiro's Analysis™ (#205)	$_____
☐ Drimogemon™ (#368)	$_____		

Other American And Japanese Cards

Other American And Japanese Cards

Market Value

- ❑ Koshiro's Analysis™ (#281) .. $_____
- ❑ Koshiro's Analysis™ (#351) .. $_____
- ❑ Koshiro's Analysis™ (#364) .. $_____
- ❑ Kuwagamon™ (#184) .... $_____
- ❑ A Lapse of Memory™ (#208) .... $_____
- ❑ Leomon™ (#343) .... $_____
- ❑ Lillymon™ (#360) .... $_____
- ❑ Losing Courage™ (#125) .... $_____
- ❑ Loss of Fighting Spirit™ (#285) .... $_____
- ❑ Mammothmon™ (#199) ..... $_____
- ❑ MegaSeadramon™ (#378) ... $_____
- ❑ Meramon™ (#355) .... $_____
- ❑ MetalGarurumon™ (#366) .. $_____
- ❑ MetalGreymon Evolution™ (#201) .... $_____
- ❑ Mimi's Kindness™ (#104) .... $_____
- ❑ Mimi's Kindness™ (#130) .... $_____
- ❑ Mimi's Kindness™ (#288) .... $_____
- ❑ Mimi's Kindness™ (#356) .... $_____
- ❑ Mimi's Kindness™ (#361) .... $_____
- ❑ Mojyamon™ (#350) .... $_____
- ❑ Monkey Song™ (#269) ..... $_____
- ❑ Monochromon™ (#296) .... $_____
- ❑ Monzaemon™ (#124) .... $_____
- ❑ Nanimon™ (#107) .... $_____
- ❑ Nanomon™ (#265) .... $_____
- ❑ Ogremon™ (#206) .... $_____
- ❑ Otamamon™ (#341) .... $_____
- ❑ Palmon™ (#372) .... $_____
- ❑ Piximon™ (#207) .... $_____
- ❑ Poisonous Air™ (#379) ..... $_____
- ❑ Power Bomb™ (#276) ..... $_____
- ❑ Powerful Sticky Sheet™ (#299) .... $_____
- ❑ Protect™ (#196) .... $_____
- ❑ Random Calculation™ (#131) .... $_____
- ❑ Raremon™ (#134) .... $_____
- ❑ Safety Campaign™ (#279) ... $_____
- ❑ Seadramon™ (#193) .... $_____
- ❑ Shut Out™ (#198) .... $_____
- ❑ SkullGreymon™ (#268) ..... $_____
- ❑ Sora's Encouragement™ (#120) .... $_____
- ❑ Sora's Encouragement™ (#185) .... $_____

Market Value

- ❑ Sora's Encouragement™ (#191) .... $_____
- ❑ Sora's Encouragement™ (#267) .... $_____
- ❑ Sora's Encouragement™ (#293) .... $_____
- ❑ Sora's Encouragement™ (#370) .... $_____
- ❑ Start Digivice!™ (#373) .... $_____
- ❑ Support Card™ (#118) ...... $_____
- ❑ Support Card™ (#121) ...... $_____
- ❑ Support Card™ (#137) ...... $_____
- ❑ Support Card™ (#212) ...... $_____
- ❑ Support Card™ #217 ...... $_____
- ❑ Support Card™ (#278) ...... $_____
- ❑ Taichi's Encouragement™ (#106) .... $_____
- ❑ Taichi's Encouragement™ (#183) .... $_____
- ❑ Taichi's Encouragement™ (#188) .... $_____
- ❑ Taichi's Encouragement™ (#263) .... $_____
- ❑ Taichi's Encouragement™ (#346) .... $_____
- ❑ Team Power +10™ (#298) ... $_____
- ❑ Team Power +15™ (#200) ... $_____
- ❑ Team Power +20™ (#115) ... $_____
- ❑ Tentomon™ (#111) .... $_____
- ❑ Togemon™ (#181) .... $_____
- ❑ Tyrannomon™ (#371) .... $_____
- ❑ Unimon™ (#262) .... $_____
- ❑ Vaccine Stun™ (#102) ...... $_____
- ❑ Vademon™ (#287) .... $_____
- ❑ Vamdemon™ (#113) .... $_____
- ❑ Virus Removal Program™ (#180) .... $_____
- ❑ Virus Stun™ (#219) .... $_____
- ❑ Vortex Of Chaos™ (#376) .. $_____
- ❑ Vortex Of Hell™ (#292) ... $_____
- ❑ WereGarurumon™ (#283) .. $_____
- ❑ WereGreymon Evolution™ (#197) .... $_____
- ❑ Wizardmon™ (#195) .... $_____
- ❑ Yamato's Crisis™ (#133) .... $_____
- ❑ Yamato's Crisis™ (#284) .... $_____
- ❑ Yamato's Crisis™ (#340) .... $_____
- ❑ Yamato's Crisis™ (#374) .... $_____
- ❑ Zudomon™ (#128) .... $_____

Page Totals:	How Many	Total Value

SUPER BROMAIDO (JAPANESE)

These gorgeous jumbo-sized Japanese cards are sold in packages of eight. Three types of cards make up the 65-card set: silver, holofoil and regular. All of these cards are numbered and assigned a Digimon power value, making it possible to use them in Digi-battle play.

	Market Value		Market Value
☐ Agumon™ (#11)	$_____	☐ Kokotorimon™ (#62)	$_____
☐ Agumon™ (#34)	$_____	☐ Koromon™ (#59)	$_____
☐ Andromon™ (#46)	$_____	☐ Kuwagamon™ (#38)	$_____
☐ Angemon™ (#4)	$_____	☐ Leomon™ (#37)	$_____
☐ Bakemon™ (#63)	$_____	☐ Meramon™ (#28)	$_____
☐ Birdramon™ (#2)	$_____	☐ Mojyamon™ (#42)	$_____
☐ Birdramon™ (#32)	$_____	☐ Monochromon™ (#19)	$_____
☐ Biyomon™ (#3)	$_____	☐ Monzaemon™ (#31)	$_____
☐ Biyomon™ (#20)	$_____	☐ Motimon™ (#50)	$_____
☐ Black Gear™ (#58)	$_____	☐ Numemon™ (#54)	$_____
☐ Bukamon™ (#65)	$_____	☐ Ogremon™ (#41)	$_____
☐ Centarumon™ (#33)	$_____	☐ Palmon™ (#12)	$_____
☐ Chuumon™ (#44)	$_____	☐ Palmon™ (#35)	$_____
☐ Devimon™ (#26)	$_____	☐ Patamon™ (#6)	$_____
☐ Digivice™ (#51)	$_____	☐ Patamon™ (#25)	$_____
☐ Drimogemon™ (#61)	$_____	☐ Piximon™ (#43)	$_____
☐ Elecmon™ (#48)	$_____	☐ Seadramon™ (#56)	$_____
☐ Etemon™ (#36)	$_____	☐ Shellmon™ (#52)	$_____
☐ Frigimon™ (#47)	$_____	☐ SkullGreymon™ (#1)	$_____
☐ Gabumon™ (#14)	$_____	☐ SkullGreymon™ (#21)	$_____
☐ Gabumon™ (#39)	$_____	☐ Sukamon™ (#49)	$_____
☐ Garurumon™ (#10)	$_____	☐ Tanemon™ (#55)	$_____
☐ Garurumon™ (#22)	$_____	☐ Tentomon™ (#9)	$_____
☐ Gazimon™ (#53)	$_____	☐ Togemon™ (#8)	$_____
☐ Gomamon™ (#15)	$_____	☐ Togemon™ (#29)	$_____
☐ Greymon™ (#7)	$_____	☐ Tokomon™ (#60)	$_____
☐ Greymon™ (#17)	$_____	☐ Tsunomon™ (#64)	$_____
☐ Ikkakumon™ (#5)	$_____	☐ Tyrannomon™ (#18)	$_____
☐ Ikkakumon™ (#23)	$_____	☐ Unimon™ (#24)	$_____
☐ Kabuterimon™ (#13)	$_____	☐ Whamon™ (#57)	$_____
☐ Kabuterimon™ (#27)	$_____	☐ Yokomon™ (#45)	$_____

Page Totals:	How Many	Total Value

Future Releases

Use this page to record future Digimon releases.

Digimon™	Value	How Many	Total Value

Page Total: | How Many | Total Value

Future Releases

Use this page to record future Digimon releases.

Digimon™	Value	How Many	Total Value

Page Total: | How Many | Total Value

Total Value Of My Collection

Record your collection here by adding the totals from the bottom of each Value Guide page.

Battle Card Starter Set

Page Number	How Many	Total Value
Page 31		
Page 32		
Page 33		
Page 34		
Page 35		
Page 36		
Page 37		
Page 38		
Page 39		
Page 40		
Page 41		
Page 42		
Page 43		
Page 44		
Page 45		
Page 46		

Battle Card Starter Set Series 2

Page Number	How Many	Total Value
Page 47		
Page 48		
Page 49		
Page 50		
Page 51		
Page 52		
Page 53		
Page 54		
Page 55		

Booster Card Series 1 & 2

Page Number	How Many	Total Value
Page 56		
Page 57		
Subtotal		

Booster Card Series 1 & 2

Page Number	How Many	Total Value
Page 58		
Page 59		
Page 60		
Page 61		
Page 62		
Page 63		
Page 64		
Page 65		
Page 66		
Page 67		
Page 68		
Page 69		
Page 70		
Page 71		
Page 72		
Page 73		
Page 74		
Page 75		
Page 76		
Page 77		
Page 78		
Page 79		
Page 80		
Page 81		
Page 82		
Page 83		
Page 84		

Booster Card Series 3

Page Number	How Many	Total Value
Page 85		
Subtotal		

Page Total:	How Many	Total Value

Total Value Of My Collection

Record your collection here by adding the totals from the bottom of each Value Guide page.

Booster Card Series 3		
Page Number	How Many	Total Value
Page 86		
Page 87		
Page 88		
Page 89		
Page 90		
Page 91		
Page 92		
Page 93		
Page 94		
Page 95		

American Trading Cards		
Page 96		
Page 97		
Page 98		
Page 99		
Page 100		
Page 101		
Page 102		
Page 103		
Page 104		
Page 105		
Page 106		
Page 107		
Page 108		
Page 109		
Page 110		

Trading Collection Light Series 1		
Page 111		
Page 112		
Subtotal		

Trading Collection Light Series 1		
Page Number	How Many	Total Value
Page 113		
Page 114		
Page 115		
Page 116		
Page 117		

Trading Collection Light Series 2		
Page 118		
Page 119		
Page 120		
Page 121		
Page 122		
Page 123		
Page 124		
Page 125		
Page 126		
Page 127		
Page 128		
Page 129		
Page 130		
Page 131		

Other American & Japanese Cards		
Page 132		
Page 133		
Page 134		
Page 135		

Future Releases		
Page 136		
Page 137		
Subtotal		

Grand Total:	How Many	Total Value

The Pro-Digi-ous Secondary Market

If you've already exhausted the supply of Digimon cards at your local store, you may not know where to turn when trying to fill in any holes in your Digimon card collection. Exploring your secondary market options can put you in touch with the card you want, and usually at a reasonable price.

The Internet is your best tool for finding the cards you need on the secondary market, with on-line auctions being a good starting point for your search. Collectors and retailers alike often post listings for single cards they have for sale. If you don't like the selection of cards you find on the auction sites, try searching on-line stores that specialize in trading and game cards.

By searching the Internet, you will find many other Digimon products besides cards. Much Digimon merchandise is still only available in Japan, but this does not necessarily mean it is out of your reach. Many Internet stores deal specifically in Japanese cards, toys and games. If you decide to go this route, spend wisely, since Japanese products are often pricier than their American counterparts because of the costs necessary to import these items.

If you'd like to see first-hand the merchandise you plan on buying, consider attending a card show. While the number of merchants won't be as large as what you would find on the Internet, there should still be more than enough Digimon products to satisfy you. These shows are often listed in the classified section of your local newspaper.

With these tips in mind, no Digimon should be out of your reach. Even if you desire an extremely rare gold "Leomon," you'll find that the secondary market can put you in touch with more Digimon than you ever imagined existed in the whole Digi-world!

Digimon Is Everywhere!

You've mastered the Digi-Battle Card Game. You've amassed complete sets of both series of trading cards, including the rare gold cards. You were first in line at your local trading card store when Booster Card Series 2 was released. You can even recite the dialogue to every episode of the animated series. Do you think that you have seen everything that's out there in regard to Digi-merchandise?

Yes?

Think again.

The world of Digimon goes far deeper than just trading cards and cartoons. There are also action figures, figurines, video games, clothes, fingerboards, plush Digi-critters and many more items available to satisfy your Digimon cravings.

In The Beginning . . .

While Digimon may seem like a new phenomenon, its roots go back to the virtual pet craze that swept Japan and the United States in the late 1990s. Digimon was introduced in Japan in 1997 and instantly appealed to kids who were looking for a virtual pet that was more action-oriented than the peaceful Tamagotchi virtual pets. With the Digimon virtual pet's unique "dock n' rock" feature (allowing two different Digimon virtual pets to battle it out), children were scrambling to train their Digimon to fight other children's Digimon.

The purpose of the Digimon virtual pet is to raise your Digimon from an egg to a powerful fighting machine such as MetalGreymon or Teddymon. There are multiple characters your Digimon can become based on how much you feed, battle and rest it.

Digimon virtual pets may be hard to find on U.S. toy store shelves, but in Japan the craze never went away, and, in fact, saw several adaptations and evolutions. In addition to several new versions of the Digimon virtual pet, Bandai also released other Digi-games, such as Digimon Pendulum and the Digivice.

The Digimon Pendulum improves upon the technology of the older Digimon virtual pets, while the Digivice is modeled after the devices used by the Digi-destined in the animated television series. The Digivice also incorporates a pedometer feature that counts the number of steps you walk. As your steps increase, your Digimon encounters more Digimon to battle. It's almost like traveling the Digi-world alongside your Digimon!

Where The Action Is

Even though there are many great products available only in Japan, Digimon is beginning to conquer the U.S. market as well, with several licensed products that capture the excitement of the Digimon phenomenon. Some of these products are currently on the market, while others are soon to be released. So keep watching your local toy store shelves for the latest and greatest in Digimon merchandise.

If you like action figures, Digimon provides you with plenty to choose from. The largest of these are the Digivolving action figures, which provide 5 inches of transforming fun. With only a few simple steps, you can Digi-volve Kabuterimon into MegaKabuterimon. Other characters available include Greymon (into MetalGreymon), Garurumon (into WereGarurumon), Patamon (into Angemon) and Birdramon (into Garudamon). As a special bonus, these Digivolving figures also come with a foil trading card that cannot be found anywhere else.

The Digivolving figures may be kings of the hill size-wise, but there are also 2.5-inch Action Feature DigiMonsters, that, like their name implies, pack an action-filled wallop. Eighteen of the most popular Digimon have 2.5-inch likenesses. For fans of the cartoon, the eight Digi-destined will soon be joining the ranks of the 2.5-inch Action Feature line, so you'll soon be able to partner them up with their Digimon.

Part of the fun of owning action figures is pitting them against each other in battle. But when you get the urge for a Digi-battle, it can sometimes be frustrating if you have nobody to fight against. Collectible Digimon Sets solve this problem for you by including between four and six 1.5-inch figurines in each set.

And for all those who've ever talked to their Digimon action figures and wished they could talk back, now you can stop wishing. Digimon Talking Figures are here and they include Agumon, Gabumon and Patamon, who repeat phrases from the cartoon show.

Read All About It!

If action figures aren't your bag, Digimon is now a comic book! You can relive your favorite animated adventures in the first four issues of the 12-issue series by Dark Horse Comics. Future issues will contain all-new stories created especially for the comic.

If you don't want to just read about Digimon, the Digimon sticker activity books and giant coloring and activity books offer hours of enjoyment and are perfect for rainy-day fun. Digimon tattoo activity books and Digimon storybooks are also available (parents, don't worry, the tattoos are only temporary).

Once you've colored in pictures of all your favorite Digimon and Digi-destined, hang them on the fridge with Digimon refrigerator magnets. Choose from magnets featuring the seven original Digi-destined kids and their companion Digimon. Mom and Dad will be so proud of their budding artists!

A Change Of Pace

For those who like collectibles, All 4 Fun Toys is releasing a series of Digimon Collector's Coins for you to collect and trade with your friends. Just don't try spending them at your local toy store!

While we're on the subject of coins, where will you put all the money that you are saving up to buy these great products? Easy! In a Digimon piggy bank, of course. The seven characters available include Tanemon, Bukamon, Koromon, Tsunomon, Motimon, Tokomon and Yokomon.

After School Special

The first day of school can be a fun day, if you go wearing your Digimon clothes and accessories. There are some great items out now that make it possible to sport Digimon apparel from head to toe! For instance, Digimon shoes and sneakers are being produced by Brown Shoe Company's popular Buster Brown division of children's footwear. Complete the look with one of several Digimon T-shirts, while Digimon backpacks "watch your back" as you walk the school halls between classes. When the lunch bell rings, take your insulated Digimon lunch bag out of your backpack and enjoy your meal.

Speaking of school, if you ever missed an episode of "Digimon: Digital Monsters" because you were busy studying or doing homework, you can catch up on what you missed with Digimon videos. Two volumes are currently available. The first volume, "Digimon: So It Begins" contains the first three episodes of the television series, while "Digimon Vol. 2" contains episodes four through six. A special 6-minute video is available in the Collectable Digimon Kit. This kit also comes with a poster and one of six unique 1.5-inch figures.

In addition to television screens, Digimon will be invading American video-game screens with the release of "Digimon World" for the Sony PlayStation. Just make sure you get your homework done before you play it.

ODDS AND ENDS

Digimon and skateboards? What an irresistible combination! The Digimon dX Mini-Skateboards have one great advantage over the other types of fingerboards available – these mini-skateboards also come with a pint-sized Digimon that doubles as a keychain. Twelve Digimon are ready to perform a wide array of stunts and tricks. Be on the lookout for more boards and characters to follow.

Also on the market are Digimon Micro Playsets, which come with one character figure and a miniature Digimon. The three playsets even transform into Digimon when you are finished playing.

JAPANESE MERCHANDISE

Are you suffering from Digi-product overload yet? No? Good, because there is a whole other world of merchandise available in

Digimon Is Everywhere!

Japan. Some of these goods may eventually be sold in the United States, while others will probably remain exclusive to Japan.

Japan has taken the collectible card game to the next level with the Card Tactics device. Looking like a cross between a calculator and a virtual pet, this "computer" lets you use your Card Tactics cards in game play against another friend using the Card Tactics device.

Another technological marvel is Bandai's Wonder Swan, a handheld, single-player video game much like Nintendo's Game Boy. There is a Digimon video game already available for this portable gaming system. The Special Package Digital Monster Version Wonder Swan comes with both the Wonder Swan game unit and the Digimon game in one box, so you can jump right in and start playing the Digimon game immediately.

For those who prefer traditional board games over computer games, the Digimon Hexa-plate System game is a perfect choice. This game combines the strategy of the card game with the play mechanics of a board game.

In addition to cards, Digimon stickers are also popular in Japan. These stickers provide power, speed and strength ratings for the characters. The sticker set consists of 75 regular stickers, 18 gold stickers and nine metal-etching stickers.

For collectors of action figures, Digivolving figures are available in Japan and are similar to their U.S. counterparts, although Japanese collectors have seven figures to choose from compared to the five available in the United States – they also get WarGreymon and MetalGarurumon.

COLLECTOR'S
VALUE GUIDE™

Action Feature Digimon figures can also be found in Japan. Some Japanese Action Feature figures, like Gatomon, are not yet available in America. Judging by Gatomon's popularity as Kari's Digimon, it should see release in the United States soon.

Japan has also seen the release of 30 mini Digimon figures that come in small cages. These figures are also available in collector packs.

Sometimes Digimon don't want to fight, they just want to be hugged. Plush characters are available in 12-inch and 6-inch sizes. These plush critters are not yet being sold in American toy stores, but stay on the lookout for these cuddly companions.

Collecting Japanese products can be frustrating because there is so much out there, but not much comprehensive information about it or one place to find it all. However, these items are not out of reach, even if you aren't planning a trip to Japan. Many Japanese products eventually become released as U.S. products. The Internet can also put you in touch with collectors and distributors who have these hard-to-find Japanese toys. By chatting with Japanese youngsters who collect Digimon, you may be able to trade some of your U.S. products for their Japanese products. A final caveat: Remember to always use caution when dealing with people you don't know on the Internet.

Digi-Dictionary

It should come as no surprise that a foreign land such as the Digi-world has its own language. The following terms are often uttered during Digimon conversations. Learn them and use them!

Black Gears – a circular, black device created by Devimon that controls good Digimon to doing its evil bidding.

Crest – represents a particular trait such as sincerity or reliability; activated whenever a Digi-destined exhibits this attribute.

Dark Network – a far-reaching system of cables that allows Etemon to spy on and obtain information about anyone anywhere in the Digi-world.

Digi-destined – the eight chosen children who have been summoned from Earth to save the Digi-world from evil.

Digimon – a shortening of the term "digital monsters."

Digivice – handy, portable device that can Digi-volve Digimon, destroy Black Gears and ward off evil Digimon.

Digi-world – a digital world, parallel to our own, where the Digi-destined meet all sorts of Digimon.

File Island – where the Digi-destined are first transported.

In-Training – usually refers to a weak Digimon that has not yet Digi-volved and that often becomes emotionally attached to one particular human.

Server – continent in the Digi-world.

Tag – when fit into the crest, enables the Digimon to Digi-volve to its ultimate level.

American Digimon Card Checklist

Check off which American cards you have and which cards you still need to acquire from the Digimon Battle and Trading card sets. The cards are listed in numerical order within each set.

Battle Card Starter Set

- ❑ Agumon™ .... (St-01)
- ❑ Greymon™ .... (St-02)
- ❑ Biyomon™ .... (St-03)
- ❑ Birdramon™ .... (St-04)
- ❑ Gabumon™ .... (St-05)
- ❑ Garurumon™ .... (St-06)
- ❑ Tentomon™ .... (St-07)
- ❑ Kabuterimon™ .... (St-08)
- ❑ Palmon™ .... (St-09)
- ❑ Togemon™ .... (St-10)
- ❑ Gomamon™ .... (St-11)
- ❑ Ikkakumon™ .... (St-12)
- ❑ Patamon™ .... (St-13)
- ❑ Angemon™ .... (St-14)
- ❑ Nanimon™ .... (St-15)
- ❑ Unimon™ .... (St-16)
- ❑ Centarumon™ .... (St-17)
- ❑ Kunemon™ .... (St-18)
- ❑ Dokugumon™ .... (St-19)
- ❑ Musyamon™ .... (St-20)
- ❑ Kimeramon™ .... (St-21)
- ❑ Rockmon™ .... (St-22)
- ❑ Gotsumon™ .... (St-23)
- ❑ Otamamon™ .... (St-24)
- ❑ Tortomon™ .... (St-25)
- ❑ Starmon™ .... (St-26)
- ❑ Gekomon™ .... (St-27)
- ❑ MegaKabuterimon™ .... (St-28)
- ❑ Triceramon™ .... (St-29)
- ❑ Piximon™ .... (St-30)
- ❑ Okuwamon™ .... (St-31)
- ❑ SkullGreymon™ .... (St-32)
- ❑ HerculesKabuterimon™ ... (St-33)
- ❑ SaberLeomon™ .... (St-34)
- ❑ Dolphmon™ .... (St-35)
- ❑ Coelamon™ .... (St-36)
- ❑ Octomon™ .... (St-37)
- ❑ Zudomon™ .... (St-38)
- ❑ MarineDevimon™ .... (St-39)
- ❑ Pukumon™ .... (St-40)
- ❑ Candlemon™ .... (St-41)
- ❑ DemiDevimon™ .... (St-42)
- ❑ Apemon™ .... (St-43)
- ❑ Wizardmon™ .... (St-44)
- ❑ Bakemon™ .... (St-45)
- ❑ Mammothmon™ .... (St-46)
- ❑ WereGarurumon™ .... (St-47)
- ❑ SkullMeramon™ .... (St-48)
- ❑ Red Offensive™ .... (St-49)
- ❑ Yellow Offensive™ .... (St-50)
- ❑ Green Offensive™ .... (St-51)
- ❑ Blitz™ .... (St-52)
- ❑ Metal Attack™ .... (St-53)
- ❑ Counter Attack!™ .... (St-54)
- ❑ To Champion™ .... (St-55)
- ❑ Ultra Digivolve™ .... (St-56)
- ❑ Downgrade™ .... (St-57)
- ❑ Digi-Duel™ .... (St-58)
- ❑ Digivice Red™ .... (St-59)
- ❑ Digivice Green & Yellow™ .... (St-60)
- ❑ Digivice Red & Green™ ... (St-61)
- ❑ Digivice Yellow™ .... (St-62)

COLLECTOR'S VALUE GUIDE™

Battle Card Booster Set Series 1 & 2

- MetalGreymon™ .... (Bo-01)
- Devimon™ .... (Bo-02)
- Leomon™ .... (Bo-03)
- Ogremon™ .... (Bo-04)
- Meramon™ .... (Bo-05)
- Seadramon™ .... (Bo-06)
- Frigimon™ .... (Bo-07)
- ShogunGekomon™ ..... (Bo-08)
- Shellmon™ .... (Bo-09)
- Drimogemon™ .... (Bo-10)
- Andromon™ .... (Bo-11)
- Monochromon™ .... (Bo-12)
- Kuwagamon™ .... (Bo-13)
- Mojyamon™ .... (Bo-14)
- Gatomon™ .... (Bo-15)
- Angewomon™ .... (Bo-16)
- Magnadramon™ .... (Bo-17)
- Ebidramon™ .... (Bo-18)
- Gorillamon™ .... (Bo-19)
- Vilemon™ .... (Bo-20)
- Minotarumon™ .... (Bo-21)
- LadyDevimon™ .... (Bo-22)
- Roachmon™ .... (Bo-23)
- Asuramon™ .... (Bo-24)
- Snimon™ .... (Bo-25)
- Jagamon™ .... (Bo-26)
- MetalEtemon™ .... (Bo-27)
- Crabmon™ .... (Bo-28)
- Syakomon™ .... (Bo-29)
- Gesomon™ .... (Bo-30)
- MegaSeadramon™ ...... (Bo-31)
- Scorpiomon™ .... (Bo-32)
- Dragomon™ .... (Bo-33)
- MarineAngemon™ ...... (Bo-34)
- MetalSeadramon™ ...... (Bo-35)
- Tapirmon™ .... (Bo-36)
- Pumpkinmon™ .... (Bo-37)
- Myotismon™ .... (Bo-38)
- Phantomon™ .... (Bo-39)
- SkullMammothmon™ .... (Bo-40)
- Boltmon™ .... (Bo-41)
- Piedmon™ .... (Bo-42)
- Fly-Trap™ .... (Bo-43)
- Coral Rip™ .... (Bo-44)
- Aquatic Attack™ .... (Bo-45)
- Fly Away™ .... (Bo-46)
- Iron Drill™ .... (Bo-47)
- Organic Enhancer™ ..... (Bo-48)
- Option Eater™ .... (Bo-49)
- Power Freeze™ .... (Bo-50)
- Even Steven™ .... (Bo-51)
- Bomb Dive™ .... (Bo-52)
- Digiruption™ .... (Bo-53)
- Depth Charge™ .... (Bo-54)
- Machinedramon™ ...... (Bo-55)
- Kokatorimon™ .... (Bo-56)
- Etemon™ .... (Bo-57)
- Whamon™ .... (Bo-58)
- Sukamon™ .... (Bo-59)
- Gazimon™ .... (Bo-60)
- Elecmon™ .... (Bo-61)
- Monzaemon™ .... (Bo-62)
- Numemon™ .... (Bo-63)
- Mamemon™ .... (Bo-64)
- MetalMamemon™ ...... (Bo-65)
- Tyrannomon™ .... (Bo-66)
- Datamon™ .... (Bo-67)
- Giromon™ .... (Bo-68)
- Megadramon™ .... (Bo-69)
- Digitamamon™ .... (Bo-70)
- Gizamon™ .... (Bo-71)
- Raremon™ .... (Bo-72)
- ExTyrannomon™ .... (Bo-73)
- Deltamon™ .... (Bo-74)
- Tuskmon™ .... (Bo-75)
- Myotismon™ .... (Bo-76)
- Gatomon™ .... (Bo-77)
- Cyclonemon™ .... (Bo-78)
- DarkTyrannomon™ ..... (Bo-79)
- MetalGreymon™ .... (Bo-80)
- Floramon™ .... (Bo-81)
- Mushroomon™ .... (Bo-82)
- Veedramon™ .... (Bo-83)
- Togemon™ .... (Bo-84)
- Kiwimon™ .... (Bo-85)
- Woodmon™ .... (Bo-86)
- RedVegiemon™ .... (Bo-87)
- AeroVeedramon™ .... (Bo-88)

American Digimon Card Checklist

COLLECTOR'S
VALUE GUIDE™

- ☐ Garudamon™ .... (Bo-89)
- ☐ Blossomon™ .... (Bo-90)
- ☐ Deramon™ .... (Bo-91)
- ☐ Cherrymon™ .... (Bo-92)
- ☐ Garbagemon™ .... (Bo-93)
- ☐ Phoenixmon™ .... (Bo-94)
- ☐ Gryphonmon™ .... (Bo-95)
- ☐ Puppetmon™ .... (Bo-96)
- ☐ Green Digivice™ .... (Bo-97)
- ☐ Red & Yellow Digivice™ .. (Bo-98)
- ☐ Crest Tag™ .... (Bo-99)
- ☐ Crest of Courage™ ..... (Bo-100)
- ☐ Crest of Reliability™ .... (Bo-101)
- ☐ Crest of Sincerity™ ..... (Bo-102)
- ☐ Crest of Friendship™ ... (Bo-103)
- ☐ Black Gears™ .... (Bo-104)
- ☐ Flood™ .... (Bo-105)
- ☐ Meat™ .... (Bo-106)
- ☐ Waterproof™ .... (Bo-107)
- ☐ Pluck™ .... (Bo-108)

American Trading Cards Series 1

- ☐ Selected Kids!™ .... (1 of 34)
- ☐ Ready For Battle! Rookies!™ .... (2 of 34)
- ☐ Digivolve! Champions!™ .... (3 of 34)
- ☐ Tai & Koromon™ .... (4 of 34)
- ☐ Matt & Tsunomon™ ..... (5 of 34)
- ☐ Sora & Yokomon™ ...... (6 of 34)
- ☐ Izzy & Motimon™ .... (7 of 34)
- ☐ Mimi & Tanemon™ ...... (8 of 34)
- ☐ Joe & Bukamon™ .... (9 of 34)
- ☐ T.K. & Tokomon™ ..... (10 of 34)
- ☐ Agumon™ .... (11 of 34)
- ☐ Gabumon™ .... (12 of 34)
- ☐ Biyomon™ .... (13 of 34)
- ☐ Tentomon™ .... (14 of 34)
- ☐ Palmon™ .... (15 of 34)
- ☐ Gomamon™ .... (16 of 34)
- ☐ Patamon™ .... (17 of 34)
- ☐ Kuwagamon™ .... (18 of 34)
- ☐ Greymon™ .... (19 of 34)
- ☐ Garurumon™ .... (20 of 34)
- ☐ Seadramon™ .... (21 of 34)
- ☐ Monochromon™ .... (22 of 34)
- ☐ Birdramon™ .... (23 of 34)
- ☐ Meramon™ .... (24 of 34)
- ☐ Kabuterimon™ .... (25 of 34)
- ☐ Togemon™ .... (26 of 34)
- ☐ Ikkakumon™ .... (27 of 34)
- ☐ Leomon™ .... (28 of 34)
- ☐ Ogremon™ .... (29 of 34)
- ☐ Devimon™ .... (30 of 34)
- ☐ Frigimon™ .... (31 of 34)
- ☐ Bakemon™ .... (32 of 34)
- ☐ Angemon™ .... (33 of 34)
- ☐ Cockatrimon™ .... (34 of 34)
- ☐ Andromon™ .... (U1 of 8)
- ☐ Monzaemon™ .... (U2 of 8)
- ☐ Etemon™ .... (U3 of 8)
- ☐ SkullGreymon™ .... (U4 of 8)
- ☐ Piximon™ .... (U5 of 8)
- ☐ MetalGreymon™ .... (U6 of 8)
- ☐ WereGarurumon™ ..... (U7 of 8)
- ☐ MegaKabuterimon™ .... (U8 of 8)
- ☐ Digimon Checklist™ ..... (N/A)

AMERICAN TRADING CARDS SERIES 2

- Bonds Of Friendship!™ .... (1 of 32)
- Gennai™ .... (2 of 32)
- Kari Kamiya™ .... (3 of 32)
- DemiDevimon™ .... (4 of 32)
- Tyrannomon™ .... (5 of 32)
- Vegiemon™ .... (6 of 32)
- Gekomon™ .... (7 of 32)
- Flymon™ .... (8 of 32)
- Gatomon™ .... (9 of 32)
- Nanimon™ .... (10 of 32)
- Devidramon™ .... (11 of 32)
- Dokugumon™ .... (12 of 32)
- Gesomon™ .... (13 of 32)
- Wizardmon™ .... (14 of 32)
- Datamon™ .... (15 of 32)
- Myotismon™ .... (16 of 32)
- Vademon™ .... (17 of 32)
- Garudamon™ .... (18 of 32)
- MegaSeadramon™ ..... (19 of 32)
- SkullMeramon™ .... (20 of 32)
- Lillymon™ .... (21 of 32)
- Phantomon™ .... (22 of 32)
- Zudomon™ .... (23 of 32)
- Mammothmon™ .... (24 of 32)
- Digivolve To Ultimate!™ .... (25 of 32)
- Rip Up! Perfect Claw!™ .... (26 of 32)
- Penetrate! Evil Dimension!™ .... (27 of 32)
- Fly! The Loving Sky!™ .. (28 of 32)
- Hot Battle! Strong Courage!™ .... (29 of 32)
- Crash! Street Battle!™ .... (30 of 32)
- Violent Shock! Decisive Battle!™ .. (31 of 32)
- Assault! Messenger From The Dark!™ .. (32 of 32)
- Agumon™ .... (D1)
- Gomamon™ .... (D2)
- Kuwagamon™ .... (D3)
- Andromon™ .... (D4)
- Unimon™ .... (D5)
- Elecmon™ .... (D6)
- Drimogemon™ .... (D7)
- Gazimon™ .... (D8)
- Digitamamon™ .... (D9)
- ShogunGekomon™ .... (D10)
- Digimon Checklist™ ...... (N/A)

Alphabetical Index

This is an alphabetical listing of all the Digimon products included in the Collector's Value Guide™, including the type of card, as well as the page number on which it appears.

Adventure Tag™ . . . . Card Tactics . . 133
AeroVeedramon™ . . . . Battle . . 58
Agumon™ . . . . Battle . . 31
Agumon™ . . . . Card Tactics . . 133
Agumon™ (#11) . . . . . . Super Bromaido . . 135
Agumon™ (#34) . . . . . . Super Bromaido . . 135
Agumon™ (11 of 34) . . . . Trading . . 96
Agumon™ (D1) . . . . Trading . . 109
Aim For The Strongest
   Evolution!™ . . . . Battle . . 86
Airdramon™ . . . . Battle . . 86
Alulamon™ . . . . Battle . . 86
Am I A Leader?™ . . . . Trading . . . 111
Andromon™ (Bo-11) . . . . Battle . . 58
Andromon™ (St-78) . . . . Battle . . 49
Andromon™ . . . . Card Tactics . . 133
Andromon™ . . . . Super Bromaido . . 135
Andromon™ (U1) . . . . Trading . . 102
Andromon™ (D4) . . . . Trading . . 109
Angemon™ (St-14) . . . . Battle . . 31
Angemon™ (St-67) . . . . Battle . . 49
Angemon™ . . . . Card Tactics . . 133
Angemon™ . . . . Promotional . . 132
Angemon™ . . . . Super Bromaido . . 135
Angemon™ . . . . Trading . . 96
Angewomon™ (Bo-16) . . . . Battle . . 58
Angewomon™ (St-77) . . . . Battle . . 49
Angewomon™ . . . . Card Tactics . . 133
Antivaccine Program™ . . . . Card Tactics . . 133
Apemon™ . . . . Battle . . 32
Aquatic Attack™ . . . . Battle . . 59
Assault! Messenger From
   The Dark!™ . . . . Trading . . 103
Asuramon™ . . . . Battle . . 59
AtolaKabuterimon™ . . . . Battle . . 49
AtolaKabuterimon™ . . . . . . Card Tactics . . 133
Attack™ . . . . Card Tactics . . 133

Babamon™ . . . . Battle . . 86
Back And Front Badge™ . . . Card Tactics . . 133
Bad Digimon™ . . . . Trading . . 123
Bad Monzaemon™ . . . . Battle . . 50
Bad Seadramon™ . . . . Battle . . 87
Bakemon™ . . . . Battle . . 32
Bakemon™ . . . . Super Bromaido . . 135
Bakemon™ . . . . Trading . . 96
Be Ready! Chosen
   Children!!™ . . . . Trading . . 118
Beat Him Up, Greymon!!™ . . . . Trading . . . 111
Betamon™ . . . . Battle . . 87
Big Mamemon™ . . . . Battle . . 50
Birdramon™ (St-04) . . . . Battle . . 32
Birdramon™ (St-85) . . . . Battle . . 50
Birdramon™ . . . . Card Tactics . . 133
Birdramon™ (#2) . . . . . . Super Bromaido . . 135

Birdramon™ (#32) . . . . . Super Bromaido . . 135
Birdramon™ . . . . Trading . . 96
Biyomon™ . . . . Battle . . 32
Biyomon™ . . . . Card Tactics . . 133
Biyomon™ (#3) . . . . Super Bromaido . . 135
Biyomon™ (#20) . . . . . . Super Bromaido . . 135
Biyomon™ . . . . Trading . . 97
Black Gear™ . . . . Card Tactics . . 133
Black Gear™ . . . . Super Bromaido . . 135
Black Gears™ . . . . Battle . . 59
Blitz™ . . . . Battle . . 33
Blossomon™ . . . . Battle . . 59
Boltmon™ . . . . Battle . . 60
Bomb Dive™ . . . . Battle . . 60
Bonds Of Friendship!™ . . . . . . Trading . . 104
Brother!™ . . . . Trading . . . 111
Bukamon™ . . . . Super Bromaido . . 135
Burumeramon™ . . . . Battle . . 50

CP Transmitting
   Pump™ . . . . Card Tactics . . 133
Can I Have A Crest,
   Please?™ . . . . Trading . . . 118
Candlemon™ . . . . Battle . . 33
Centarumon™ (St-17) . . . . Battle . . 33
Centarumon™ (St-75) . . . . Battle . . 50
Centarumon™ . . . . Card Tactics . . 133
Centarumon™ . . . . Super Bromaido . . 135
Cheer Up, Joe™ . . . . Trading . . . 111
Cherrymon™ . . . . Battle . . 60
Chuumon™ . . . . Super Bromaido . . 135
Clockmon™ . . . . Battle . . 87
Cockatrimon™ . . . . Trading . . 97
Coelamon™ . . . . Battle . . 33
Cold Breath™ . . . . Card Tactics . . 133
Come On Everybody!
   Follow Me!!™ . . . . Trading . . . 118
Coral Rip™ . . . . Battle . . 60
Counter Attack!™ . . . . Battle . . 34
Counter-Attack!™ . . . . Battle . . 50
Crabmon™ . . . . Battle . . 61
Crash! Street Battle!™ . . . . Trading . . 104
Crest Of Courage™ . . . . Battle . . 61
Crest Of Friendship™ . . . . Battle . . 61
Crest Of Hope™ . . . . Battle . . 87
Crest Of Knowledge™ . . . . Battle . . 87
Crest Of Love™ . . . . Battle . . 87
Crest Of Reliability™ . . . . Battle . . 61
Crest Of Sincerity™ . . . . Battle . . 62
Crest Tag™ . . . . Battle . . 62
Cyclonemon™ . . . . Battle . . 62

Dark Network™ . . . . Battle . . 88
DarkTyrannomon™ . . . . Battle . . 62
Data – DA™ . . . . Card Tactics . . 133

153

Alphabetical Index

Data Destruction
  Program™ . . . . Card Tactics . . 133
Datamon™. . . . . Battle . . . 63
Datamon™ . . . . Trading . . 104
Deadly Foxfire™. . . . . Trading. . . 111
Deathmeramon™. . . . . Card Tactics . . 133
Deltamon™ . . . . Battle . . . 63
DemiDevimon™ . . . . Battle . . . 34
DemiDevimon™ . . . . Card Tactics . . 133
DemiDevimon™. . . . . Trading . . 104
Depth Charge™. . . . . Battle . . . 63
Deramon™. . . . . Battle . . . 63
Deterioration™ . . . . Card Tactics . . 133
Devidramon™. . . . . Battle . . . 88
Devidramon™ . . . . Card Tactics . . 133
Devidramon™. . . . . Trading . . 104
Devil Chip™ . . . . Battle . . . 88
Devimon™ (Bo-02) . . . . Battle . . . 64
Devimon™ (St-76). . . . . Battle . . . 51
Devimon™. . . . . Card Tactics . . 133
Devimon™ . . . . Super Bromaido . . 135
Devimon™ (30 of 34) . . . . Trading . . . 97
Devimon™ (P9) . . . . Trading . . 116
Devimon's Desire™ . . . . Trading. . . 111
Digi-Duel™. . . . . Battle . . . 34
Digimon Checklist™. . . . . Trading . . . 97
Digimon Checklist™. . . . . Trading . . 104
Digiruption™. . . . . Battle . . . 64
Digital Injection™ . . . . Card Tactics . . 133
Digitamamon™. . . . . Battle . . . 64
Digitamamon™ . . . . Card Tactics . . 133
Digitamamon™. . . . . Trading . . 109
Digivice™. . . . . Card Tactics . . 133
Digivice™. . . . . Super Bromaido . . 135
Digivice Green & Yellow™ . . . . . . Battle . . . 34
Digivice Red™ . . . . Battle . . . 35
Digivice Red & Green™ . . . . Battle . . . 35
Digivice Yellow™ . . . . Battle . . . 35
Digivolve! Champions!!™. . . . . Trading . . . 97
Digivolve To Ultimate!™ . . . . . Trading . . 105
Discovery Of Invader™ . . . . . . Trading. . . 112
Disregard This!™. . . . . Battle . . . 88
Do You Think You Can
  Defeat Me?™. . . . . Trading. . . 118
Dokugumon™. . . . . Battle . . . 35
Dokugumon™ . . . . Card Tactics . . 133
Dokugumon™. . . . . Trading . . 105
Dolphmon™ (St-35). . . . . Battle . . . 36
Dolphmon™ (St-68). . . . . Battle . . . 51
Don't Eat!!™ . . . . Trading. . . 112
Don't Ignore Us!!™ . . . . Trading. . . 112
Don't Worry About Me.
  Just Go . . .™ . . . . Trading. . . 118
Downgrade™. . . . . Battle . . . 36
Drag Into Water!™. . . . . Battle . . . 51
Dragomon™ . . . . Battle . . . 64
Dream Is Gone™. . . . . Trading. . . 112
Drimogemon™ . . . . Card Tactics . . 133
Drimogemon™. . . . . Battle . . . 65
Drimogemon™. . . . . Super Bromaido . . 135
Drimogemon™. . . . . Trading . . 109

Ebidramon™ . . . . Battle . . . 65
Elecmon™. . . . . Battle . . . 65
Elecmon™. . . . . Super Bromaido . . 135
Elecmon™. . . . . Trading . . 110
Elecmon™ . . . . Card Tactics . . 133
Emergency Provisions™
  (#182) . . . . Card Tactics . . 133
Emergency Provisions™
  (#342) . . . . Card Tactics . . 133
Emergency Provisions
  (small)™ (#264). . . . . Card Tactics . . 133
Energy Loss™ . . . . Card Tactics . . 133
Etemon™. Battle . . . 65
Etemon™. . . . . Card Tactics . . 133
Etemon™. . . . . Super Bromaido . . 135
Etemon™ . . . . Trading . . 102
Even Steven™ . . . . Battle . . . 66
Everybody's Here! Our Team
  Power Is Full Now!!™ . Card Tactics . . 133
Evolved Palmon!
  Togemon!!™ . . . . Trading. . . 112
ExTyrannomon™. . . . . Battle . . . 66

Fake Betamon™ . . . . Battle . . . 88
Fake Drimogemon™ . . . . Battle . . . 88
Final Battle!™. . . . . Trading. . . 112
Fire Breath™ . . . . Card Tactics . . 133
Flood™ . . . . Battle . . . 66
Floppy Disk™. . . . . Battle . . . 89
Floramon™ . . . . Battle . . . 66
Fly Away™ . . . . Battle . . . 67
Fly! The Loving Sky!™. . . . . . Trading . . 105
Fly-Trap™. . . . . Battle . . . 67
Flymon™. Battle . . . 89
Flymon™. . . . . Card Tactics . . 133
Flymon™. . . . . Trading . . 105
Frigimon™. . . . . Battle . . . 67
Frigimon™. . . . . Card Tactics . . 133
Frigimon™ . . . . Super Bromaido . . 135
Frigimon™. . . . . Trading . . . 97

Gabumon™. . . . . Battle . . . 36
Gabumon™ . . . . Card Tactics . . 133
Gabumon™ (#14) . . . . . Super Bromaido . . 135
Gabumon™ (#39) . . . . . Super Bromaido . . 135
Gabumon™. . . . . Trading . . . 98
Garbagemon™. . . . . Battle . . . 67
Garudamon™. . . . . Battle . . . 68
Garudamon™ . . . . Card Tactics . . 133
Garudamon™ . . . . Promotional . . 132
Garudamon™ . . . . Trading . . 105
Garurumon™ (Bo-120) . . . . Battle . . . 89
Garurumon™ (St-06) . . . . Battle . . . 36
Garurumon™ (St-88) . . . . Battle . . . 51
Garurumon™ . . . . Card Tactics . . 133
Garurumon™ (#10) . . . . Super Bromaido . . 135
Garurumon™ (#22) . . . . Super Bromaido . . 135
Garurumon™ . . . . Trading . . . 98
Gatomon™ (Bo-15) . . . . Battle . . . 68
Gatomon™ (Bo-77) . . . . Battle . . . 68
Gatomon™ . . . . Card Tactics . . 133
Gatomon™ . . . . Trading . . 105
Gazimon™. . . . . Battle . . . 68

Alphabetical Index

Gazimon™. . . . . Card Tactics . . 133
Gazimon™. . . . . Super Bromaido . . 135
Gazimon™ . . . . Trading. . . 110
Gekomon™. . . . . Battle . . . 37
Gekomon™. . . . . Trading . . 106
Gelemon™. . . . . Battle . . . 89
Gennai™ . . . . Card Tactics . . 133
Gennai™. . . . . Trading . . 106
Gesomon™ . . . . Battle . . . 69
Gesomon™. . . . . Trading . . 106
Get Power Together!™ . . . . Trading. . . 112
Giromon™. . . . . Battle . . . 69
Gizamon™. . . . . Battle . . . 69
Glowing Digivice!!™ . . . . Trading. . . 112
Go! Kabuterimon!!™. . . . . Trading. . . 112
Go! MetalGreymon!!™ . . . . Trading. . . 118
Going Berserk™ . . . . Card Tactics . . 133
Going To A New
   Continent!™. . . . . Trading. . . 113
Gomamon™. . . . . Battle . . . 37
Gomamon™. . . . . Card Tactics . . 133
Gomamon™. . . . . Super Bromaido . . 135
Gomamon™ (16 of 34) . . . . Trading . . . 98
Gomamon™ (D2) . . . . Trading . . 110
Gorillamon™. . . . . Battle . . . 69
Gotsumon™ (St-23). . . . . Battle . . . 37
Gotsumon™ (St-62). . . . . Battle . . . 51
Green Digivice™. . . . . Battle . . . 70
Green Offensive™. . . . . Battle . . . 37
Greymon™ (St-02) . . . . Battle . . . 38
Greymon™ (St-91) . . . . Battle . . . 51
Greymon™ . . . . Card Tactics . . 133
Greymon™ (#7). . . . . . . Super Bromaido . . 135
Greymon™ (#17). . . . . . Super Bromaido . . 135
Greymon™. . . . . Trading . . . 98
Gryphonmon™ . . . . Battle . . . 70
Guardmon™ . . . . Battle . . . 89

Hagurumon™. . . . . Battle . . . 52
Hand From The Dark™ . . . . Battle . . . 89
Hangyomon™ . . . . Battle . . . 52
Have A Mega Flame!!™ . . . . Trading. . . 113
He's Coming!!™. . . . . Trading. . . 113
HerculesKabuterimon™. . . . . Battle . . . 38
Hikari™ (P8). . . . . Trading . . 123
Hikari™ (Puzzle Card 64). . . . . . Trading . . 124
Hikari™ (Puzzle Card 65). . . . . . Trading . . 124
Hikari™ (Puzzle Card 66). . . . . . Trading . . 124
Hikari™ (Puzzle Card 67). . . . . . Trading . . 124
Hikari™ (Puzzle Card 68). . . . . . Trading . . 124
Hikari™ (Puzzle Card 69). . . . . . Trading . . 124
Hikari™ (Puzzle Card 70). . . . . . Trading . . 124
Hikari™ (Puzzle Card 71). . . . . . Trading . . 124
Hikari™ (Puzzle Card 72). . . . . . Trading . . 124
Hot Battle! Strong Courage!™ . . Trading . . 106
Hurry Up! The Gate
   Is Closing!!™. . . . . Trading. . . 119

I Can't Evolve. . .™ . . . . Trading. . . 113
I Can't Lose™. . . . . Trading. . . 119
I Can't Lose Like This!™ . . . . Battle . . . 52
I Don't Want To Go!!™. . . . . Trading. . . 119
I Feel Hurt™ . . . . Battle . . . 52

I Have Been Waiting For You,
   Chosen Children™ . . . . Trading. . . 119
I Have To Go . . .™. . . . . Trading. . . 119
I Protect Koshiro!™ . . . . Trading. . . 119
I Will Help Yamato!™. . . . . Trading. . . 113
I Will Kill You!™ . . . . Trading . . 120
I Will Save You This Time!!™ . . Trading. . . 113
I Will Take The Crests From
   The Children™. . . . . Trading . . 120
IceDevimon™ . . . . Battle . . . 52
Icemon™. . . . . Battle . . . 90
Igamon™. . . . . Battle . . . 90
Ikkakumon™. . . . . Battle . . . 38
Ikkakumon™. . . . . Card Tactics . . 133
Ikkakumon™ (#5) . . . . . Super Bromaido . . 135
Ikkakumon™ (#23) . . . . Super Bromaido . . 135
Ikkakumon™. . . . . Trading . . . 98
Illegal Drink™. . . . . Card Tactics . . 133
I'll Never Fail To Get A
   Crest!!™ . . . . Trading. . . 119
I'll Save You Now, Joe!!™ . . . . . Trading. . . 119
I'm The Strongest Digimon™ . . . Trading. . . 119
Instant Hospitalization™ . . . Card Tactics . . 133
Iron Drill™ . . . . Battle . . . 70
It Is Great To Be Able To
   Fly!™ . . . . Battle . . . 52
Izzy & Motimon™. . . . . Promotional . . 132
Izzy & Motimon™ . . . . Trading . . . 98

Jagamon™. . . . . Battle . . . 70
Jijimon™. . . . . Battle . . . 90
Joe™ (P7) . . . . Trading . . 123
Joe™ (Puzzle Card 55) . . . . Trading . . 125
Joe™ (Puzzle Card 56) . . . . Trading . . 125
Joe™ (Puzzle Card 57) . . . . Trading . . 125
Joe™ (Puzzle Card 58) . . . . Trading . . 125
Joe™ (Puzzle Card 59) . . . . Trading . . 125
Joe™ (Puzzle Card 60) . . . . Trading . . 125
Joe™ (Puzzle Card 61) . . . . Trading . . 125
Joe™ (Puzzle Card 62) . . . . Trading . . 125
Joe™ (Puzzle Card 63) . . . . Trading . . 125
Joe & Bukamon™ . . . . Promotional . . 132
Joe & Bukamon™ . . . . Trading . . . 99
Joe's Partner™ . . . . Trading . . 116

Kabuterimon™ (St-08). . . . . Battle . . . 38
Kabuterimon™ (St-66). . . . . Battle . . . 53
Kabuterimon™ . . . . Card Tactics . . 134
Kabuterimon™ (#13) . . . Super Bromaido . . 135
Kabuterimon™ (#27) . . . Super Bromaido . . 135
Kabuterimon™. . . . . Trading . . . 99
Kamenolimon™. . . . . Battle . . . 53
Kari Kamiya™. . . . . Trading . . 106
Kimeramon™. . . . . Battle . . . 39
Kiwimon™ . . . . Battle . . . 71
Knightmon™ . . . . Battle . . . 90
Kokatorimon™. . . . . Battle . . . 71
Kokatorimon™ . . . . Card Tactics . . 134
Kokatorimon™ . . . . Super Bromaido . . 135
Kokuwamon™. . . . . Battle . . . 53
Koromon™ . . . . Super Bromaido . . 135
Koshiro™ (P4) . . . . Trading . . 123
Koshiro™ (Puzzle Card 28). . . . . Trading . . 126

155

Alphabetical Index

Koshiro™ (Puzzle Card 29)..... Trading .. 126	MegaSeadramon™............ Battle ... 73
Koshiro™ (Puzzle Card 30)..... Trading .. 126	MegaSeadramon™........ Card Tactics .. 134
Koshiro™ (Puzzle Card 31)..... Trading .. 126	MegaSeadramon™........... Trading .. 107
Koshiro™ (Puzzle Card 32)..... Trading .. 126	Meramon™................. Battle ... 74
Koshiro™ (Puzzle Card 33)..... Trading .. 126	Meramon™............ Card Tactics .. 134
Koshiro™ (Puzzle Card 34)..... Trading .. 126	Meramon™.......... Super Bromaido .. 135
Koshiro™ (Puzzle Card 35)..... Trading .. 126	Meramon™................. Trading ... 99
Koshiro™ (Puzzle Card 36)..... Trading .. 126	Metal Attack™............... Battle ... 40
Koshiro's Analysis™ (#110). Card Tactics .. 134	MetalEtemon™............... Battle ... 74
Koshiro's Analysis™ (#205). Card Tactics .. 134	MetalGarurumon™............ Battle ... 91
Koshiro's Analysis™ (#281). Card Tactics .. 134	MetalGarurumon™...... Card Tactics .. 134
Koshiro's Analysis™ (#351). Card Tactics .. 134	MetalGreymon™ (Bo-01)...... Battle ... 74
Koshiro's Analysis™ (#364). Card Tactics .. 134	MetalGreymon™ (Bo-80)...... Battle ... 74
Koshiro's Partner™............ Trading... 116	MetalGreymon™ (Bo-115)..... Battle ... 91
Kunemon™ (St-18)............. Battle ... 39	MetalGreymon™.......... Promotional .. 132
Kunemon™ (St-63)............. Battle ... 53	MetalGreymon™.............. Trading .. 102
Kuwagamon™ (Bo-13)......... Battle ... 71	MetalGreymon Evolution™. Card Tactics .. 134
Kuwagamon™ (St-73).......... Battle ... 53	MetalMamemon™............. Battle ... 75
Kuwagamon™............ Card Tactics .. 134	MetalSeadramon™ (Bo-35)..... Battle ... 75
Kuwagamon™....... Super Bromaido .. 135	MetalSeadramon™ (St-87)..... Battle ... 53
Kuwagamon™ (18 of 34)...... Trading ... 99	MetalTyrannomon™........... Battle ... 91
Kuwagamon™ (D3) .... Trading... 110	Meteoritemon™.............. Battle ... 91
	Mimi™ (P6)................. Trading .. 123
LadyDevimon™............... Battle ... 71	Mimi™ (Puzzle Card 46)...... Trading .. 127
Lapse Of Memory, A™ .... Card Tactics .. 133	Mimi™ (Puzzle Card 47)...... Trading .. 127
Leave It To Me!™............. Trading... 113	Mimi™ (Puzzle Card 48)...... Trading .. 127
Leomon™ (Bo-03)............. Battle ... 72	Mimi™ (Puzzle Card 49)...... Trading .. 127
Leomon™ (St-72)............. Battle ... 53	Mimi™ (Puzzle Card 50)...... Trading .. 127
Leomon™............... Card Tactics .. 134	Mimi™ (Puzzle Card 51)...... Trading .. 127
Leomon™........... Super Bromaido .. 135	Mimi™ (Puzzle Card 52)...... Trading .. 127
Leomon™.................. Trading ... 99	Mimi™ (Puzzle Card 53)...... Trading .. 127
Leomon And Ogremon™...... Trading... 116	Mimi™ (Puzzle Card 54)...... Trading .. 127
Let's Find The Rest Of	Mimi & Tanemon™....... Promotional .. 132
Our Friends!™........... Trading .. 120	Mimi & Tanemon™........... Trading .. 100
Let's Go Find The Last	Mimi's Kindness™ (#104).. Card Tactics .. 134
One!!™................. Trading .. 120	Mimi's Kindness™ (#130).. Card Tactics .. 134
Let's Join Forces!™........... Trading... 113	Mimi's Kindness™ (#288).. Card Tactics .. 134
Let's Sneak In!™............ Trading .. 120	Mimi's Kindness™ (#356).. Card Tactics .. 134
Libolumon™.................. Battle ... 54	Mimi's Kindness™ (#361).. Card Tactics .. 134
Lillymon™.................. Battle ... 90	Mimi's Partner™............. Trading .. 116
Lillymon™............. Card Tactics .. 134	Minotarumon™............... Battle ... 75
Lillymon™................. Trading .. 106	Mojyamon™ (Bo-14).......... Battle ... 75
Losing Courage™....... Card Tactics .. 134	Mojyamon™ (St-90).......... Battle ... 54
Loss Of Fighting Spirit™... Card Tactics .. 134	Mojyamon™........... Card Tactics .. 134
	Mojyamon™......... Super Bromaido .. 135
Machinedramon™ (Bo-55)...... Battle ... 72	MoliShellmon™............... Battle ... 91
Machinedramon™ (Bo-136)..... Battle ... 91	Monkey Song™......... Card Tactics .. 134
MagnaAngemon™............. Battle ... 90	Monochromon™.............. Battle ... 76
Magnadramon™.............. Battle ... 72	Monochromon™........ Card Tactics .. 134
Mamemon™.................. Battle ... 72	Monochromon™..... Super Bromaido .. 135
Mammothmon™.............. Battle ... 39	Monochromon™............. Trading .. 100
Mammothmon™...... Card Tactics .. 134	Monzaemon™................ Battle ... 76
Mammothmon™............. Trading .. 107	Monzaemon™.......... Card Tactics .. 134
MarineAngemon™............. Battle ... 73	Monzaemon™....... Super Bromaido .. 135
MarineDevimon™............. Battle ... 39	Monzaemon™.............. Trading .. 102
Matt & Tsunomon™....... Promotional .. 132	Motimon™.......... Super Bromaido .. 135
Matt & Tsunomon™.......... Trading ... 99	Mushroomon™............... Battle ... 76
Meat™.................... Battle ... 73	Musyamon™................. Battle ... 40
Megadramon™ (Bo-69)......... Battle ... 73	My Crest Doesn't Glow!™..... Trading .. 120
Megadramon™ (St-94)......... Battle ... 54	My Tag Is Glowing!™....... Trading .. 120
MegaKabuterimon™........... Battle ... 40	Myotismon™ (Bo-38)......... Battle ... 76
MegaKabuterimon™ ..... Promotional .. 132	Myotismon™ (Bo-76)......... Battle ... 77
MegaKabuterimon™.......... Trading .. 102	Myotismon™............... Trading .. 107

Alphabetical Index

Nanimon™ . . . . Battle . . . 40	Random Calculation™ . . . . . Card Tactics . . 134
Nanimon™ . . . . Card Tactics . . 134	Raremon™ . . . . Battle . . . 80
Nanimon™ . . . . Trading . . 107	Raremon™ . . . . Card Tactics . . 134
Nanomon™ . . . . Card Tactics . . 134	Ready For Battle! Rookies!!™ . . Trading . . 100
Numemon™ . . . . Battle . . . 77	Red Offensive™ . . . . Battle . . . 43
Numemon™ . . . . Super Bromaido . . 135	RedKokatorimon™ . . . . Battle . . . 92
	RedVegiemon™ . . . . Battle . . . 80
Octomon™ . . . . Battle . . . 41	Red & Yellow Digivice™ . . . . Battle . . . 80
Ogremon™ (Bo-04) . . . . Battle . . . 77	Resurrection From The Dark!!™ . . Battle . . . 92
Ogremon™ (St-89) . . . . Battle . . . 54	Rip Up! Perfect Claw!™ . . . . . . Trading . . 108
Ogremon™ . . . . Card Tactics . . 134	Rival Is Vaccine!, A™ . . . . Battle . . . 55
Ogremon™ . . . . Super Bromaido . . 135	Roachmon™ . . . . Battle . . . 80
Ogremon™ . . . . Trading . . 100	Rockmon™ . . . . Battle . . . 43
Oh My God! They Found	
Us!!™ . . . . Trading . . 120	Saberdolamon™ . . . . Battle . . . 92
Oh, No! A Monster!!™ . . . . Trading . . 120	SaberLeomon™ . . . . Battle . . . 44
Ohkuwamon™ . . . . Battle . . . 54	Safety Campaign™ . . . . . Card Tactics . . 134
Okuwamon™ . . . . Battle . . . 41	Saikemon™ . . . . Battle . . . 93
Option Eater™ . . . . Battle . . . 77	Save Mimi!!™ . . . . Trading . . 121
Organic Enhancer™ . . . . Battle . . . 78	Scorpiomon™ . . . . Battle . . . 81
Otamamon™ . . . . Battle . . . 41	Seadramon™ . . . . Battle . . . 81
Otamamon™ . . . . Card Tactics . . 134	Seadramon™ . . . . Card Tactics . . 134
	Seadramon™ . . . . Super Bromaido . . 135
Palmon™ (St-09) . . . . Battle . . . 41	Seadramon™ . . . . Trading . . 101
Palmon™ (St-111) . . . . Battle . . . 54	Seed Of Health™ . . . . Battle . . . 93
Palmon™ . . . . Card Tactics . . 134	Seed Of Speed™ . . . . Battle . . . 93
Palmon™ (#12) . . . . Super Bromaido . . 135	Seed Of Strength™ . . . . Battle . . . 93
Palmon™ (#35) . . . . Super Bromaido . . 135	Selected Kids!™ . . . . Trading . . 101
Palmon™ . . . . Trading . . 100	Sender Should Be Here!, The™ . . Trading . . 121
Panjamon™ . . . . Battle . . . 55	Shellmon™ . . . . Battle . . . 81
Patamon™ . . . . Battle . . . 42	Shellmon™ . . . . Super Bromaido . . 135
Patamon™ (#6) . . . . Super Bromaido . . 135	ShogunGekomon™ . . . . Battle . . . 81
Patamon™ (#25) . . . . . Super Bromaido . . 135	ShogunGekomon™ . . . . Trading . . 110
Patamon™ . . . . Trading . . 100	Shut Out™ . . . . Card Tactics . . 134
Penetrate! Evil Dimension!™ . . . Trading . . 107	SkullGreymon™ . . . . Battle . . . 44
Penmon™ . . . . Battle . . . 92	SkullGreymon™ . . . . Card Tactics . . 134
Phantomon™ . . . . Battle . . . 78	SkullGreymon™ (#1) . . . Super Bromaido . . 135
Phantomon™ . . . . Trading . . 107	SkullGreymon™ (#21) . . Super Bromaido . . 135
Phoenixmon™ . . . . Battle . . . 78	SkullGreymon™ . . . . Trading . . 103
Piedmon™ . . . . Battle . . . 78	SkullMammothmon™ . . . . Battle . . . 82
Piximon™ . . . . Battle . . . 42	SkullMeramon™ (St-48) . . . . Battle . . . 44
Piximon™ . . . . Card Tactics . . 134	SkullMeramon™ (St-71) . . . . Battle . . . 55
Piximon™ . . . . Super Bromaido . . 135	SkullMeramon™ . . . . Trading . . 108
Piximon™ . . . . Trading . . 103	Snimon™ . . . . Battle . . . 82
PlatinaSukamon™ . . . . Battle . . . 92	SnowAgumon™ . . . . Battle . . . 93
Pluck™ . . . . Battle . . . 79	Sora™ (P3) . . . . Trading . . 123
Plug-In Attack A™ . . . . Battle . . . 42	Sora™ (Puzzle Card 19) . . . . . . Trading . . 128
Plug-In B™ . . . . Battle . . . 42	Sora™ (Puzzle Card 20) . . . . . . Trading . . 128
Plug-In Defense C™ . . . . Battle . . . 43	Sora™ (Puzzle Card 21) . . . . . . Trading . . 128
Plug-In S™ . . . . Battle . . . 55	Sora™ (Puzzle Card 22) . . . . . . Trading . . 128
PoisonKunemon™ . . . . Battle . . . 92	Sora™ (Puzzle Card 23) . . . . . . Trading . . 128
Poisonous Air™ . . . . Card Tactics . . 134	Sora™ (Puzzle Card 24) . . . . . . Trading . . 128
Power Bomb™ . . . . Card Tactics . . 134	Sora™ (Puzzle Card 25) . . . . . . Trading . . 128
Power Freeze™ . . . . Battle . . . 79	Sora™ (Puzzle Card 26) . . . . . . Trading . . 128
Powerful Sticky Sheet™ . . . Card Tactics . . 134	Sora™ (Puzzle Card 27) . . . . . . Trading . . 128
Preshiomon™ . . . . Battle . . . 55	Sora & Yokomon™ . . . . Promotional . . 132
Pretend You're Stuffed	Sora & Yokomon™ . . . . Trading . . 101
Animals™ . . . . Trading . . 121	Sora's Encouragement™
Protect™ . . . . Card Tactics . . 134	(#120) . . . . Card Tactics . . 134
Pukumon™ . . . . Battle . . . 43	Sora's Encouragement™
Pumpkinmon™ . . . . Battle . . . 79	(#185) . . . . Card Tactics . . 134
Puppetmon™ . . . . Battle . . . 79	Sora's Encouragement™
	(#191) . . . . Card Tactics . . 134

157

Alphabetical Index

Sora's Encouragement™
  (#267) . . . . Card Tactics . . 134
Sora's Encouragement™
  (#293) . . . . Card Tactics . . 134
Sora's Encouragement™
  (#370) . . . . Card Tactics . . 134
Sora's Partner™ . . . . Trading. . . 116
Spiral Sword™ . . . . Trading. . . 113
Starmon™ . . . . Battle . . . 44
Start Digivice!™ . . . . Card Tactics . . 134
Stop! Greymon!!™. . . . . Trading . . . 121
Sukamon™ . . . . Battle . . . 82
Sukamon™ . . . . Super Bromaido . . 135
Super Evolution!
  Garudamon!!™. . . . . Trading . . . 121
Support Card™ (#118) . . . . . Card Tactics . . 134
Support Card™ (#121) . . . . . Card Tactics . . 134
Support Card™ (#137) . . . . . Card Tactics . . 134
Support Card™ (#212) . . . . . Card Tactics . . 134
Support Card™ (#217) . . . . . Card Tactics . . 134
Support Card™ (#278) . . . . . Card Tactics . . 134
Syakomon™ . . . . Battle . . . 82

T.K. & Tokomon™. . . . . Promotional . . 132
T.K. & Tokomon™ . . . . Trading . . . 101
Tai & Koromon™ . . . . Promotional . . 132
Tai & Koromon™ . . . . Trading . . . 101
Taichi™ (P1). . . . . Trading . . . 123
Taichi™ (Puzzle Card 01) . . . . . Trading . . . 129
Taichi™ (Puzzle Card 02) . . . . . Trading . . . 129
Taichi™ (Puzzle Card 03) . . . . . Trading . . . 129
Taichi™ (Puzzle Card 04) . . . . . Trading . . . 129
Taichi™ (Puzzle Card 05) . . . . . Trading . . . 129
Taichi™ (Puzzle Card 06) . . . . . Trading . . . 129
Taichi™ (Puzzle Card 07) . . . . . Trading . . . 129
Taichi™ (Puzzle Card 08) . . . . . Trading . . . 129
Taichi™ (Puzzle Card 09) . . . . . Trading . . . 129
Taichi, Dangerous!!™. . . . . Trading. . . 114
Taichi's Encouragement™
  (#106) . . . . Card Tactics . . 134
Taichi's Encouragement™
  (#183) . . . . Card Tactics . . 134
Taichi's Encouragement™
  (#188) . . . . Card Tactics . . 134
Taichi's Encouragement™
  (#263) . . . . Card Tactics . . 134
Taichi's Encouragement™
  (#346) . . . . Card Tactics . . 134
Taichi's Partner™ . . . . Trading. . . 117
Take That!™ . . . . Trading . . . 121
Takeru™ (P5) . . . . Trading . . . 123
Takeru™ (Puzzle Card 37) . . . . . Trading . . . 130
Takeru™ (Puzzle Card 38) . . . . . Trading . . . 130
Takeru™ (Puzzle Card 39) . . . . . Trading . . . 130
Takeru™ (Puzzle Card 40) . . . . . Trading . . . 130
Takeru™ (Puzzle Card 41) . . . . . Trading . . . 130
Takeru™ (Puzzle Card 42) . . . . . Trading . . . 130
Takeru™ (Puzzle Card 43) . . . . . Trading . . . 130
Takeru™ (Puzzle Card 44) . . . . . Trading . . . 130
Takeru™ (Puzzle Card 45) . . . . . Trading . . . 130
Takeru, Where Are You!!™ . . . . . Trading. . . 114
Takeru's Partner™. . . . . Trading. . . 117
Tanemon™. . . . . Super Bromaido . . 135

Tankmon™ . . . . Battle . . . 55
Tapirmon™ . . . . Battle . . . 83
Team Power +10™ . . . . . . Card Tactics . . 134
Team Power +15™ . . . . . . Card Tactics . . 134
Team Power +20™ . . . . . . Card Tactics . . 134
Tentomon™ . . . . Battle . . . 45
Tentomon™ . . . . Card Tactics . . 134
Tentomon™ . . . . Super Bromaido . . 135
Tentomon™ . . . . Trading . . . 101
The Sender Should Be Here!™ . . Trading . . . 121
There Is A Deserted
  Factory!™ . . . . Trading. . . 114
This Is A Return Match!™. . . . . . . Battle . . . 56
This Is It! Is This Further
  Evolution?!™. . . . . Trading . . . 121
This Is My Crest!™. . . . . Trading . . . 121
This Scene . . . I've Seen
  It Before™ . . . . Trading . . . 121
This Sounds Nice™. . . . . Trading. . . 114
To Champion™ . . . . Battle . . . 45
Togemon™ (Bo-84) . . . . Battle . . . 83
Togemon™ (St-10). . . . . Battle . . . 45
Togemon™ . . . . Card Tactics . . 134
Togemon™ (#8) . . . . Super Bromaido . . 135
Togemon™ (#29) . . . . . . Super Bromaido . . 135
Togemon™ . . . . Trading . . . 102
Togemon Vs. Monzaemon™. . . . Trading. . . 114
Tokomon™ . . . . Super Bromaido . . 135
Tortomon™ . . . . Battle . . . 45
ToyAgumon™ . . . . Battle . . . 93
Training Manual™. . . . . Battle . . . 56
Triceramon™ . . . . Battle . . . 46
Tsuchidalumon™ . . . . Battle . . . 94
Tsukaimon™ . . . . Battle . . . 94
Tsunomon™ . . . . Super Bromaido . . 135
Tuskmon™ . . . . Battle . . . 83
Tyrannomon™ . . . . Battle . . . 83
Tyrannomon™ . . . . Card Tactics . . 134
Tyrannomon™ . . . . Super Bromaido . . 135
Tyrannomon™ . . . . Trading . . . 108

Ultra Digivolve™. . . . . Battle . . . 46
Unimon™ (St-16) . . . . Battle . . . 46
Unimon™ (St-74) . . . . Battle . . . 56
Unimon™ . . . . Card Tactics . . 134
Unimon™ . . . . Super Bromaido . . 135
Unimon™ . . . . Trading. . . 110

Vaccine Stun™. . . . . Card Tactics . . 134
Vademon™ . . . . Battle . . . 94
Vademon™ . . . . Card Tactics . . 134
Vademon™ . . . . Trading . . . 108
Vamdemon™ . . . . Card Tactics . . 134
Vamilimon™ . . . . Battle . . . 94
Veedramon™ . . . . Battle . . . 84
Vegiemon™ . . . . Battle . . . 94
Vegiemon™ . . . . Trading . . . 108
VenomMyotismon™ . . . . Battle . . . 56
Vilemon™ . . . . Battle . . . 84
Violent Shock! Decisive
  Battle!™. . . . . Trading . . . 108
Virus Removal Program™ . . Card Tactics . . 134
Virus Stun™ . . . . Card Tactics . . 134

Alphabetical Index

Vortex Of Chaos™........ Card Tactics .. 134
Vortex Of Hell™ .... Card Tactics .. 134

Wait, Both Of You!™ .... Trading... 114
WarGreymon™ .... Battle ... 56
Waterproof™ .... Battle ... 84
We Are Honor Students™ .... Battle ... 94
We Are Saved ...™ .... Trading... 114
Welcome To Pagumon
    Village!™................ Trading... 122
Welcome To Tokomon
    Village™ .... Trading... 114
WereGarurumon™................ Battle ... 46
WereGarurumon™........ Card Tactics .. 134
WereGarurumon™......... Promotional .. 132
WereGarurumon™............. Trading... 103
WereGreymon Evolution™ . Card Tactics .. 134
Wh ... Who Are You?™....... Trading... 114
Whamon™ (Bo-58) .... Battle ... 84
Whamon™ (St-92).............. Battle ... 56
Whamon™.......... Super Bromaido .. 135
What? A Public Telephone??™.. Trading... 115
What Are You?!™............. Trading... 115
What Should We Do ... ?™.... Trading .. 122
Where Is Everybody?™ .... Trading... 115
Where Is The Eighth Child?™... Trading .. 122
Why Did You Evolve?™....... Trading... 115
Why Is A Teddy Bear
    Attacking Us!™.......... Trading... 115
Winning Percentage 40%!™
    (Bo-104) .... Battle ... 85
Winning Percentage 40%!™
    (Bo-155) .... Battle ... 95
Winning Percentage 40%!™
    (St-59).................. Battle ... 47
Winning Percentage 40%!™
    (St-101)................. Battle ... 57
Winning Percentage 60%!™
    (Bo-105) .... Battle ... 85
Winning Percentage 60%!™
    (Bo-156) .... Battle ... 95
Winning Percentage 60%!™
    (St-60).................. Battle ... 47
Winning Percentage 60%!™
    (St-102)................. Battle ... 57
Wizardmon™ (St-44)........... Battle ... 47
Wizardmon™ (St-70)........... Battle ... 57
Wizardmon™............ Card Tactics .. 134
Wizardmon™ .... Trading .. 109

Woodmon™.................... Battle ... 85
Work Harder!!™............. Trading .. 122
Wow!™...................... Trading... 115
Wow! They're Coming!!™..... Trading... 115

Yamato™ (P2)............... Trading .. 123
Yamato™ (Puzzle Card 10)..... Trading .. 131
Yamato™ (Puzzle Card 11)..... Trading .. 131
Yamato™ (Puzzle Card 12)..... Trading .. 131
Yamato™ (Puzzle Card 13)..... Trading .. 131
Yamato™ (Puzzle Card 14)..... Trading .. 131
Yamato™ (Puzzle Card 15)..... Trading .. 131
Yamato™ (Puzzle Card 16)..... Trading .. 131
Yamato™ (Puzzle Card 17)..... Trading .. 131
Yamato™ (Puzzle Card 18)..... Trading .. 131
Yamato's Crisis™ (#133)... Card Tactics .. 134
Yamato's Crisis™ (#284)... Card Tactics .. 134
Yamato's Crisis™ (#340)... Card Tactics .. 134
Yamato's Crisis™ (#374)... Card Tactics .. 134
Yamato's Partner™........... Trading... 117
Yellow Offensive™ .... Battle ... 47
Yes! Agumon!!™............. Trading... 115
Yes! Birdramon!!™........... Trading... 115
Yes! I'm Back!!™ .... Trading .. 122
Yokomon™ .... Super Bromaido .. 135
You Are Alive, Taichi!!™ ..... Trading .. 122
You Are An Important
    Partner!™................ Trading .. 116
You Don't Know Anything
    About Me!™ .... Trading... 116
You, Too!!™................. Trading... 116

Zudomon™ (St-38) .... Battle ... 48
Zudomon™ (St-69) .... Battle ... 57
Zudomon™ .... Card Tactics .. 134
Zudomon™.................. Trading .. 109

ACKNOWLEDGEMENTS

CheckerBee Publishing would like to extend a very special thanks to Yvette Rooney of SB Gifts and Hobbies in Middletown, NY and Joy Goodnough of Joy's Japanimation in Greensburg, PA. We would also like to thank Kevin Hall, Leisa Lee, Philip J. Murphy and Misaki Takeda, who contributed their valuable time to assist us with this book.

Catch Our Hottest Guides

CheckerBee PUBLISHING

Digimon™
Dragon Ball Z™
Fifty State Quarters
Hot Wheels®
NASCAR®
Dale Earnhardt
Jeff Gordon
Pokémon™
Ty® Beanie Babies®
Wrestling
X-Men®

COLLECTOR'S VALUE GUIDE™

And that's not all! We have 27 great titles available in stores everywhere. You gotta see them all! To find out more call toll free:
800.746.3686 or visit CollectorBee.com

Master The World Of Digimon™

If you love Digimon™, our web site is for you! Check it out today!

CollectorBee.com

- Keep up with the latest Digimon™ news!
- Trade your cards on our free Bulletin Board
- Try your luck with our contest & giveaways

306 Industrial Park Road   Middletown, CT 06457   800.746.3686   www.collectorbee.com